A STILLNESS OF THOUGHT

FINDING YOUR WAY THROUGH A DYSFUNCTIONAL AND VIOLENT CHILDHOOD TO BECOME A FULLY FUNCTIONAL, HAPPY AND SATISFIED ADULT

K. D. CANNON

Copyright © 2020 K. D. Cannon.

ALL RIGHTS RESERVED. This book contains material protected under International and Federal Copyright Laws and Treaties. Any unauthorized reprint or use of this material is prohibited. No part of this book may be reproduced or transmitted in any form or by any means, electronic or mechanical, including photocopying, recording, or by any information storage and retrieval system without express written permission from the author/publisher.

ISBN: 978-1-64184-487-1 (Paperback)
ISBN: 978-1-64184-488-8 (Hardcover
ISBN: 978-1-64184-489-5 (Ebook)

DEDICATION

To Devona Dotson-Muday, I love you!

CONTENTS

Introduction ix

A Stillness of Thought

Chapter 1   Awareness 5
Chapter 2   Trauma 6

DARKNESS....

Chapter 3   Placed in Protective Custody 11
Chapter 4   The State Police Post 14
Chapter 5   Father's Mother and Father 16
Chapter 6   Father 18
Chapter 7   Mother 20
Chapter 8   The Chakra System 23

Chapter 9	Mother and Father's Marriage	30
Chapter 10	Pills and booze	31
Chapter 11	Life with Mom and Dad	32
Chapter 12	Know Thy Self	34
Chapter 13	Knowledge of Your Tribe	40
Chapter 14	The Orphanage	45
Chapter 15	The History of American Orphanages	49
Chapter 16	Entombed	53
Chapter 17	A Child is Born!	54
Chapter 18	Boundaries	61
Chapter 19	The Effects of Domestic Violence on Children	67
Chapter 20	Adoptive Parents' Background	71
Chapter 21	Sibling Separation	75
Chapter 22	Arrival into a New Family	78
Chapter 23	House on The Lake	83
Chapter 24	Magical Thinking	85
Chapter 25	Narcissistic Parents	92
Chapter 26	What's Your Name?	97
Chapter 27	The Making of a Codependent	99
Chapter 28	Pets?	105
Chapter 29	Blackouts and Alcohol Addiction	109
Chapter 30	Healing Is on Its Way!	115
Chapter 31	An Epiphany	120

Chapter 32	The Building of a New Foundation	126
Chapter 33	Coming Full Circle	132
Chapter 34	Education, Hmmm	137
Chapter 35	The Ego's Use of Emotions	141
Chapter 36	Hold Your Friends Close, Hold Your Enemies Closer	146
Chapter 37	Bits of Wisdom Attained on the Journey	151
Chapter 38	Giving and Receiving Are the Same	153

Epilogue 159
Acknowledgements 161
References 163

INTRODUCTION

Writing this book came from Spirit, who told me many times through others and my intuition to, "Write it already!"

A great portion of A Sti*llness of Thought* is written in the first person, to help you identify yourself in parts of it.

Changing your thinking and feelings about yourself is not a road for the whimsical. It takes focused determination and unwavering faith, even when the shit is hitting the fan all around you!

My career was as a licensed manicurist, facialist and massage therapist. Professionally, I touched thousands of folks from around the world and all walks of life.

While performing my first pedicure on a client, while still in training, I felt something, not a physical thing, but something emotional. A block. It was very dark, and it felt like trauma. I gently asked her if she had been injured on that side of her body. She then proceeded to tell me the story of how her father hit her foot with a hammer!

I intuitively knew I could bring soothing comfort into clients' bodies and at the same time, if the client was open to it, suggest a new way to look at their physical issues, through what they may be thinking and feeling in their consciousness.

Over time, it became evident to me that we are all connected in consciousness!

I am not a doctor of any sort, just a person like you, walking through the life I was given, doing the best I can do to make it count for something.

This book is part of leaving my footsteps in the sand.

I had to write it because it wanted the world to know that miracles happen every day! It wanted me to ask you a question: Do you know and feel that you can be who you want to be?

It has been written in love for all my fellow humans who are searching for understanding and methods of finding solution and ease to the challenge of living in power, instead of the powerlessness of victimhood and mentality imposed in childhood.

Everyone who comes into your life — your employer, associates, spouse, lover, friends, and children — are all affected by how and what you think and feel about yourself. Your perception of life is affected by the trauma of your childhood. Unless you decide and act on it to change the way you think and feel about yourself, you will be imposing your victim thinking and attitudes, consciously or unconsciously, on every situation, person and aspect in your life. It's up to you to be who you want to be! Just sayin'.

A Stillness of Thought is written through the miracles of healing, which do not take place in linear time.

My hope is that this little book will provide the motivation needed to get you up off your couch and do something loving and kind for yourself and all those in your sphere of life!

Take what you need from this story and leave the rest; just take something and begin your part in healing your world.

Peace be with you,
K.D. Cannon
April 18, 2020

"Education is the most powerful weapon which you can use to change the world … things I learnt when I was negotiating was that until I changed myself, I could not change others."

—Nelson Mandela

A STILLNESS OF THOUGHT

I was happy with the slumber of long-ago felt emotions;
Lying in the sun, along a quietly flowing river;
As a butterfly taking flight, landing wherever was pleasing;
To taste this and that.
Now, the sun has clouded over, the river is rising
with thunderous turbulence.
The butterfly's wings are dampened by the tear drops
of the raging water.
She cannot flit the music of her wings.
She sits.
Frozen.
Remembering....

1
AWARENESS

AS SLEEP MELTS from my mind, I feel a warm glow penetrating my three-year-old body. A familiar scent and feel of a pillow cradle my head. My blue eyes slowly open to see the window just off center, to the left of the bed. Through this portal the sun is smiling its morning glow and warmth into the blue-green bedroom with glorious, laughing brightness. I'm washed in pure joy and feel the radiance of love!

I burst into laughter!
Look! I have a body!
I throw the warm covers off, jump up, and run downstairs as fast as my little feet and legs can go.
I must tell my mommy!
"I woke up alive today!

2
TRAUMA

IT'S MID-OCTOBER, THE shiny knotty-pine walls and waxed cream-colored tiled floor bounce with reflections of the afternoon sun. The living room is vibrating with the music of Elvis Presley and Johnny Cash. With my sisters, Linda and Vicki, we prance around the room with our rhythmic bodies, twirling each other, laughing, singing, dancing round our little brother, Wilson, as he plays on the floor.

Dad walks in the room, just coming home from work, asking where Mom is. Excited because he's home and out of breath from our aerobics, I tell him, "Mom's taking a nap."

We four kids, happily jabbering among ourselves, follow Dad into their bedroom.

There she is! The blankets are up to her neck. Her face is so pretty!

As dad sits down on the edge of the bed; he picks up a pair of mom's panties off the dresser, letting them hang from his fingertips, he lightly drags them over her smiling face.

Their playing mesmerizes me.

Now that I have my siblings quieted down and playing with each other in the bunk- bed back room, I move into the living room.

The house is quiet.

I sit down on the left end of the green couch, where mommy and daddy make cigarettes. I reach over, pick up a rolled cigarette and the silver lighter, flip its top, and light up.

I hear a noise; it sounds like knocking on the walls coming from mom and dad's bedroom.

I can hear them, but not their words.

Their voices sound mad.

The door handle is jiggling, but the door isn't opening.

Someone is screaming!

POW! The bedroom door slams open!

Mommy! Crawling across the hall floor into the bathroom!

She turns, in front of me, crying, blood all over her naked body!

Daddy! He just pounced from the bedroom!

He's standing over mom like a giant, kicking her and yelling swear words at her; "I'll kill you, you god damned bitch!"

She is so tiny.

With each kick, she screams out!

They are right in front of me. They don't see me because I'm hiding behind the smoke of the cigarette.

I can't breathe!

Mommy's almost to the living room door.

Mommy's screaming, crying, naked, and bleeding!

I am four years, ten months, and fifteen days old....

DARKNESS.....

3
PLACED IN PROTECTIVE CUSTODY

COMING OUT OF the blackness, I see the rooms, the furniture, and the people in shades of grays and whites. My siblings and I are in the neighbor's home, eating breakfast. They live across the street from my family's house.

The sun coming through the multiple square windows make the table and its breakfast contents glow.

I hear one of the adults say that someone is coming to pick us up and take us somewhere.

I grab Wilson, holding him on my hip, running outside the gloomy house. Daylight pierces my eyes; somehow Vicki and Linda are holding on to each of my hands as we run down the front porch steps, across the road to our empty home.

I don't know who "They" are, but I know they are coming to take us away!

I'm big and strong!

I'm on the grass!

I'm running across the cement road!

Hurrying, we pass dad's white and blue car to the side door of our house.

I open the screen door and turn the knob to our kitchen door, it's locked!

I can't see in; the green curtains are covering the window. Where is my Daddy? His car is here!

I shove my sisters under dad's car and sit Wilson on the stoop of the kitchen door, closing the screen door to hide him from whatever is coming to take us away!

All of us are bawling, tears and snot running down our faces.

The road is black.

The grass is green.

The house is grey.

The dark car is here!

I can save us!

I won't let them take us!

I'm strong!

I am magical!

I stood my ground, in the middle of the sidewalk, next to my dad's car, frightened. Strangers are taking us away from home!

I am magical! I can keep these aliens away from us!

They see us!

They're getting out of a car!

They're walking right up the sidewalk to the back door to Wilson!

They see Linda and Vicki under dad's car and fetch them out!

I run to the front of my daddy's car. They're touching me!

They pick me up like I am nothing! Can't they see how big and strong I am?

I am magical!

"Leave me alone!" I scream at them while twisting, turning, and kicking to get away from their grip on me.

I am magical!

Protesting in terror, my arms and legs whip the air. They lay me on the floor, behind the front seat of the car, and place their feet on me to hold me down.

I am four years and eleven months old.

Again, darkness blankets my mind.

4
THE STATE POLICE POST

MY HEAD HURTS; it feels funny on the inside and the outside.

Sitting on the edge of a cement swimming pool, dangling my feet in the cool blue water, in the glaring sun, I feel wavy and melting.

Everything looks fuzzy, but I feel, hear, and then see my sisters and brother beside me.

An adult, dressed in dark blue, stoops down next to me saying something about everything is going to be okay.

There's white cement for ground instead of green grass.

It's got cracks in it.

Step on a crack, break your mother's back.

There's a big square building behind us.

There's a fence around everything!

Outside the fence is a big road; I can tell because all the cars are going by so fast.

The adults with the dark blue clothes, with silver badges and a belt with a gun hanging off it, take us inside the square building and give us cold milk and cookies.

I know about guns. My daddy had some guns in the living room; knives, too. He was throwing the knives into the cream tile floor when the police came and took him away.

I feel funny.

Once more, darkness weaves through my mind.

5
FATHER'S MOTHER AND FATHER

MY FATHER'S MOTHER, Mary, was born in 1900 to Native American/Caucasian and African American parents. Her parents were born post-Civil War. Her parents had fourteen children, Grandma being the youngest.

When Grandma was four months old and her sister, Helen about two years old, Great-grandfather placed them in a Catholic orphanage because he couldn't afford to feed them. Grandmother was raised in an orphanage until she turned twenty-one.

She met John, who would become my Grandpa, the summer she was released from the orphanage. Grandpa was also estranged from his parents; I don't know if they died or something happened to their relationship as parents and child. He was raised by an aunt and uncle.

Grandpa served in Canada, during the beginning of WWI; I don't know which branch, came home from there and went directly into the U.S. armed forces. John and Mary met in the summer of 1921, after Grandpa completed his military commitment.

Grandpa was an alcoholic. Back in the day, he made his own liquor and beer.

Grandma was raised in a religious institution. She told me how the nuns would pinch and twist the skin on her face and arms when she misbehaved.

Two lonely young people, longing for love and to belong to someone and some place, they married soon after they met.

They had five children, four boys and one girl, all born before the Great Depression, which was a worldwide economic decline that lasted ten years. It began when the stock market prices fell twenty-three percent in four days in October 1929.

Grandpa worked for the auto industry. Grandma was a stay-at-home mom.

Grandpa beat his wife regularly, teaching his boys that when you hit your wife, she deserved it. Also, teaching his daughter that if she married a man who beat her, she deserved it and this was a normal way of living.

Grandpa and Grandma's youngest child and only daughter married a man who was an alcoholic. He beat her, and regularly sexually and physically abused their children. They also had four boys and a girl.

Grandma told me she caught Grandpa with a woman in their bedroom; he had tried to hide the other woman under the bed. From that day on, Grandma had lovers of her own who came to the house. Her lovers would sit with her husband and they would drink beer together while Grandma finished getting ready for her date.

My grandparents were Catholic; therefore, they didn't believe in divorce.

6
FATHER

GRANDPA BEAT MY dad with wire coat hangers and electrical cords, especially if he got into his father's homemade brew.

My father, Teats was taught to be rough and hard. Dad used swear words for everyday language. My native tongue is swearing. A habit, thank God, I have learned to let go of. I only speak this language when I feel deeply frustrated or extremely angry.

At seventeen dad joined the Merchant Marine and sailed the Great Lakes for two years. When he came off those ships, he joined the United States Navy at nineteen, during World War II.

During his Navy years, he was in China. He witnessed people getting their hands chopped off for stealing a loaf of bread. The most horrifying experience he had serving his country was when their ship moved into the shores of China, where he saw hundreds of dead female infants floating in the waters.

Dad, like his father, was an alcoholic.

When dad came out of the service, Grandpa got him a job in the same auto manufacturing plant he worked in.

Father extended his childhood training into my parents' marriage. He was conditioned in alcoholism, bar fights and wife beating.

7
MOTHER

MOM'S MOTHER WAS an alcoholic who wasn't married for years. Instead, she had boyfriends or in those days, children in those days were instructed to call them, "Uncle."

She allowed her boyfriends to molest mom.

When my mother, Delores was eight years old, she had two younger siblings, one about a year old and the other three years old. Once, when Grandma and her boyfriend wanted to go to the bar, it was winter, so they loaded the three kids in their pick-up truck. They decided to leave the children in the running vehicle while they went into the tavern to drink. The two youngest died that night, in the truck, next to my mother, from carbon monoxide poisoning. Mom didn't die because she was older, and her body could fight the effects of the murdering poison.

Mom's mother was in competition with my mom so much that when my mother became pregnant with her youngest child, Grandma got pregnant also. Therefore, my half-sister, born from mom's second marriage, has an aunt who was born the same year she was.

Delores and Teats, my parents, were both alcoholics.

After the state placed the four children from my parents' marriage in protective custody, they divorced. Mom moved to California, married Pete, another alcoholic, and had three more children, two boys and a girl. Mom would retrieve food from dumpsters of nearby restaurants to get food to feed her children. She divorced her second husband.

When my mother married her third husband, Damien, she became pregnant with her eight child, it was still born.

When I was back with my family of origin, about a year, I witnessed my mother's attitudes and behaviors with her youngest daughter, Theresa.

Mom and I were to meet at her home and go out to lunch together. She told me that she had an errand to run and if she wasn't home when I got there to wait for her in the family room, she would be back soon.

When I arrived, she wasn't there, so I went into the family room and sat down on the sofa. On the coffee table was a letter of sorts, so being alone and curious, I picked it up and read it.

Mom and Damien were having a written conversation about how mom felt that Damien wanted to have sex with Theresa. Damien told mom that he would beat my little half-sister and give her a bloody lip if that would prove to my mother that he wasn't interested in Theresa sexually!

Later in the day I get a phone call from Theresa telling me that she had ran away from home because she was afraid, she had found the letter just before going to school that day. She was relieved because I believed her, I had told her that I read the letter.

I attempted to intervene to help this little twelve-year child, I had a conversation with our mother, and she insisted that her youngest female child was going to be kicked out of their home!

I was shocked! She had already lost four of her children, why would she treat her child in this manner. From that moment on, I never had anything to do with her.

Of the last three children mom had, Delores and her husband, Damien were extremely emotionally and physically abusive to her youngest son, Sam and the youngest of her seven children, Theresa. The eldest of these last three, Dan, was subjected to beatings given by their stepfather, Damien. Somehow mom idolized Dan, he was protected somewhat from being mistreated and given many opportunities to excel as a teenager, therefore, he was not an easy target as his two youngest siblings were for abuse. Even today when Theresa tries to talk to him about her childhood, he tells her she is lying. Dan is in denial and has his mother on a pedestal.

Mom perpetuated the violence and mistreatments of her childhood on her seven children.

8
THE CHAKRA SYSTEM

> "It is up to us, how we explore the great wonders in our body, its life force, and subtle centers we call "CHAKRAS." We can either deny that they exist or learn to understand, work, and awaken them in order to live a more fulfilling life on Planet Earth."
> —Raju Ramanathan, *Souls from Mercury: Chakra Magic: Empowering Relationships*

WHEN A FAMILY is shattered, the children abused, and the whereabouts of siblings and parents' unknown, the chakra system is severely affected.

The chakra system originated in India between 1500 and 500 BCE in the oldest text called the Vedas. There are many Chakra systems, or "wheels" in our bodies, but the Western world has been focused on the seven mentioned below.

Chakras are the circular vortexes of energy that are placed in seven different points on the spinal column, and all the seven chakras are energetically connected to the various organs and glands within the body.

Whenever a chakra is disrupted or blocked, its life energy also gets blocked. When the harmonious balance of the seven chakras is disrupted or damaged, it can cause several problems in our lives, affecting our physical health, emotional health, and our mental state of mind.

In Sanskrit, the Root Chakra defines our relationship with Mother Earth. It influences our passion, creativity, youthfulness, vitality and most importantly, our basic survival instincts, stability, and security. This includes our basic needs such as food, water, shelter, safety, as well as our emotional needs of interconnection, and being fearless.

It is also symbolic of our physical strength, our sexuality, and the flight-or-fight response that tends to activate within our body when we sense danger.

1. The **Root Chakra** is in the small region just between the genitals and the anus, at the base of the spine, and it's all about grounding. It represents rigidity and stability and it has a foundational energy that provides a stable structure on which the chakra system rests. Direct emotions associated with the Root chakra are security and survival and relating to the world. Red is its color, which also indicates a need for logic, realistic thinking and order in our lives. Its element is Earth; its associated animal is the Elephant.

At the emotional level, the deficiencies or imbalance in the first chakra are related to an excessive feeling of insecurity and constantly living in survival mode. It may be hard for you to feel safe in the world and everything looks like a potential risk. Desire for security may dominate your thoughts, such as a job situation, physical safety, shelter, and health. When the Root chakra is blocked, behaviors are mainly ruled by fear. It is connected to your sense of smell. The Root chakra also represents your tribe and tribal belief systems. If you witnessed domestic violence, physical and emotional abuse, your Root chakra is most likely out of balance and needs clearing. This can be done through a Reiki healer and/or meditation.

Do you live in survival mode?

2. The **Sacral Chakra** is symbolic of water elements present within your body. Its color is orange. It is located about three inches below your belly button. This chakra tends to impact our ability to be happy and joyful, compassionate, creative, and passionate. It influences our desires, sexuality, and reproductive functions. It is connected to our sense of taste.

Does feeling happy and joyful appeared elusive to you? Is it difficult for you to focus on your desires? Do you feel sexually uncomfortable and have experienced reproductive problems?

3. The **Solar Plexus Chakra** is regarded as one of the most powerful chakras and has profound influences on our personal power. It represents our personal abilities and powers, and it influences our personal and professional success. Its color is yellow. This symbolizes its connection with energy and fire and can charge emotional energies. It is located about three inches above your belly button and can be associated with intuition. When the Solar Plexus chakra is in harmonious balance, we are more energetic, active, confident, and forthcoming, with a cheerful disposition that allows us to respect ourselves and others. The Solar Plexus chakra relates to our sense of sight and its energy relates to our adrenal glands.

Respect this chakra! It guides you through life when you listen to it.

Do you sabotage yourself often by questioning your intuition? News flash! Your intuition will not explain itself to you! So, don't bother asking it why it wants you to do what it wants you to do. The explanation may come after you have listened and followed its lead. It will gently lead you in the right direction. When we follow our intuition, we attain harmonious balance, have more energy, become more active and confident, which leads to a cheerful disposition because we gain respect for ourselves, which spills over into respect for others. It's amazing how that works!

4. The **Heart Chakra** is associated with the element of air within our body and has the most profound influence on our professional and personal relationships. Its location is in the heart region of our chest. Green denotes its color. If this chakra is weak and fragile, we infuse our relationships with negative emotions, distrust, and wrath. The Heart Chakra impacts our sense of touch and is connected to the lymph and thymus glands.

Have you discovered yet that when you don't allow yourself to feel your emotions, that your heart closes? You may know the feeling: lack of compassion for others, grumpy, a downer to be with. Have you noticed that when you allow yourself to feel your feelings, you gain trust and can approach life from a more positive attitude? This is because you have opened your Heart Chakra. You live life in color instead of black and white.

5. The **Throat Chakra** symbolizes our true inner voice, our ability to communicate with others. Blue in color. It's associated with our abilities to listen and empathize. In harmonic balance, it allows us to enjoy a beautiful voice, artistic potential, creative expression, and to reach a higher spiritual awareness. Its energy is connected to the throat, jaws, neck vertebrae, thyroid, teeth, ears, and esophagus. When in balance, the Throat Chakra in human beings has a powerful artistic potential, ability to meditate freely and can utilize energy effectively.

Has your throat felt like it suddenly had a catch in it for a minute or two when you told someone about the "secrets" of your childhood? Have you ever started coughing for no reason at all when you were having a conversation with someone? This is the energy of your Throat Chakra guiding you into a new way of using your power of speech.

To begin clearing your Throat Chakra, think about what you truly want to say before you say it. This will take some practice. When you speak your truth in integrity most the time, (we all mess up occasionally) you will not have to concern yourself with telling untruths or misrepresenting yourself. Often, we can't remember the lies we speak and sometimes when we lie, we must tell another lie to cover the first one we told. I don't know about you, but that's not something I want to spend my energy on. Don't fool yourself, others know when their being lied to.

6. The **Brow or Third Eye Chakra** is the center of knowledge; it is symbolized by the color indigo. It is located a little above and between the eyebrows. It's associated with our thoughts, ability to rationalize, to use logic and conduct an analysis to reach reasonable conclusions. When our Third Eye Chakra is in balance, we can be very charming and charismatic, we don't fear death or trouble and we also have powerful telepathic abilities. This chakra is connected to the pituitary and pineal gland and is also associated with elements of telepathic communication and electricity.

The electricity that runs through your brain is enough to light up a city the size of New York — or destroy it. You are connected to all humans and all of life through your consciousness and when your Third Eye Chakra is balanced, you know stuff. For instance, you've probably had the experience where you were thinking of someone and lo and behold, you ran into them shopping or they called you! That's telepathic communication!

7. The **Crown Chakra** relates to the element of light and is in the soft area of your skull. Its color is deep purple, representing the colors red, (matter), and blue, (spiritual energy). As the Root Chakra connects us to Mother Earth, the Crown Chakra is our connection to the Source. This energy center enables

you to experience spiritual growth. It disperses the Universal energy or life force into the other six chakras. It's responsible for the transcendence of your limitations and is the meeting point between the physical body, Source, and your soul. When the Crown Chakra is blocked there may be feelings of isolation, emotional distress, a feeling of being disconnected from everyone and everything. Color and sense are associated with this chakra; its element is oneness with all. Through the Crown Chakra your intuitive mind grows in wisdom.

When your Crown Chakra is blocked, you may feel depressed, isolated, and disconnected, not only from others, but from yourself and Source as well.

When this chakra is in balance, you will feel connected to yourself, family, friends, work associates, and your Source. You may even feel light, playful, and joyous.

The Seven Major Chakras

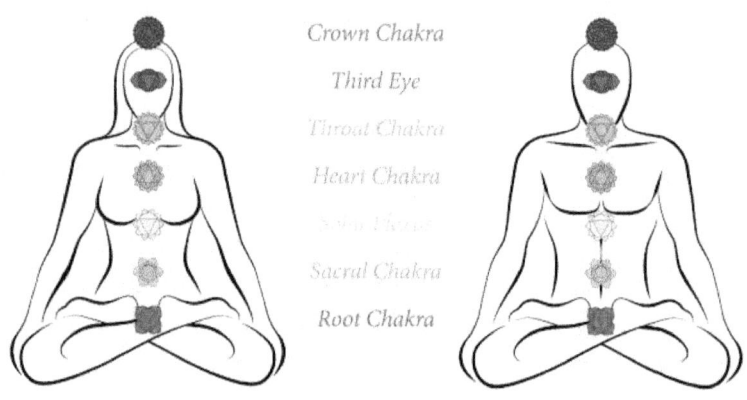

This chart is by Alissa Monroe https://www.psychics4today.com/7-chakras

Maybe you could consider using this meditation, "Harmonic Vibrations of Crystal Singing Bowls" by Crystal

Voices. You can purchase it from Amazon for $9.95. It has the sounds of crystal bowls playing in the background. This is a wonderful tool for working with your Chakra system.

> "When we develop the heart chakra, we begin to influence the surroundings with our spiritual presence.
>
> "When we develop the communication chakra, we begin to influence the country with our spiritual presence.
>
> "When we develop the seventh chakra, we begin to influence the world with our spiritual presence without doing anything."
>
> —Swami Dhyan Giten, *Presence - Working from Within. The Psychology of Being*

9
MOTHER AND FATHER'S MARRIAGE

MOM AND DAD knew each other as children, they grew up on the same East Side of town, Flint, Michigan.

After Dad returned from the armed forces, he and mom got married. She was seventeen years old, he was twenty-two years old.

Mom had been conditioned as a child to expect to be physically hurt by men; Dad had been taught to be a wife beater, and both were alcoholics.

He told me stories about him smashing her head into the dashboard of their car if he didn't like her behavior when they were out socializing.

Once, I asked him, "Why did you beat mom that one day?"

"I got really pissed at her that day at work, I don't know why, and decided when I got home, I was going to kill her." He lowered his face over his cup of hot, black coffee and took a sip.

10
PILLS AND BOOZE

Pills and booze,

Mom and dad's mind in a snooze.

Slaps and punches, loud voice and screams; bunches.

The walls sad and dark, looming loss, real and stark.

The sounds of sirens, men in uniform, handcuffs, and guns, the family torn.

Grownups in and out in a rush, fear locking me in a gush.

Neighbors all in their yards,

Us, the four kids, hiding under dad's car.

11
LIFE WITH MOM AND DAD

I WAS THE first child born to my parents, arriving on New Year's Day. My father told me I was the tenth child born in Genesee County in 1953

I have been told that I was deeply wanted by my parents. Even though there was much physical and emotional violence between my mother and father, I always felt loved by them.

I would fix breakfast for mom: cereal, toast and coffee. I was responsible for changing the younger siblings' diapers, feeding them and taking care of them. I wasn't even five years old yet.

Mom would lock us out of the house all day, it had to be clean and orderly when dad arrived home from work or he would give her a thrashing.

I pulled Vicki, Linda, and Wilson around in the Red Flyer wagon or take them into the little woods next to our house to play near the trickling stream. Sometimes I would steal milk and bread off the neighbors' porches to feed us.

We would go visit my dad's parents and my cousins would be there too. In my grandparents' back yard there was a garage;

the oldest male cousin would corner me behind it and touch me in a way that didn't feel right. I can still see the paint peeling from rotting wood and smell its musty, oily odor.

Dad sometimes would throw knives into the living-room floor or wave a gun around. Once, the police came in our house and took him away in their car.

He was in handcuffs, sitting in the back seat of a black and white car with a round red light flashing on its top. I went up to the car, on the side where dad was, and he said, "Kathy, take care of the family while I'm gone."

"I will, daddy."

I don't have any memories of my father abusing me physically, only of him gently playing with us.

I have memories of mother slamming my head against something wooden, and her giving my one-year old brother a plastic dry-cleaning bag while in his crib. I walked into his room and saw that he was wrapped in plastic, struggling. I remember firemen coming and saving his life.

I was told later, as an adult, that when my sister was ten days old, my father came home and saw that she had a black eye! He asked my mother what happened, she told him that Vicki wouldn't stop crying so she punched her to get her to shut up. Then dad proceeded to punch mom.

Dad told me he would come home from work, run his fingers along the frames over the doors and if there was dust there, he would beat mom.

But I remember only the hammering dad gave mom the day that destroyed our family.

Most of the brutal acts of violence he administered to my mother I witnessed are hidden in the files of my sub-conscious mind. And later I out pictured my parents' brutal relationship through a marriage that nearly cost me my life.

I only lived with them for the first five years of my life! Scary, huh?

12
KNOW THY SELF

> "There is no easy walk to freedom anywhere, and many of us will have to pass through the valley of the shadow of death again and again before we reach the mountaintop of our desires."
>
> —Nelson Mandela

THE WEIGHT OF deep and heavy feelings you experience from reading this book and doing these written exercises will lighten and transform into strength for you. Knowing how you processed your childhood, in other words, the attitudes and beliefs you developed about yourself back there, is giving you a very deep knowledge about yourself. And knowledge is power because then you have choices that you didn't have before! Most of the time in victim attitudes, there is the belief, there is no other choice. This is bullshit; there are always other choices we can make!

Maybe you have shadow memories that surface in your conscious mind.

If you have some of this going on, take an unlined sheet of paper and a pencil, use a colored one if you prefer, drawing the shadow thoughts that float across your mind. If you use this method, it is not about being an artist, it can be stick images or very childlike drawings. The idea here is to acknowledge these images, because usually they are something you witnessed or experienced, but your ego mind is protecting your conscious mind from the emotional impact of realizing this really happened. Another way to do this is use colored construction paper. Cut out the images using black paper and paste them to another color of paper. Intellectualizing your feelings will not be helpful here or anywhere in this work; you must "feel" your feelings, allow them to surface. Yes, it will feel like your feelings will destroy you and the life you've created, but that is your ego talking, not your spirit. Your spirit has led you here!

Your feelings want to be acknowledged. It is natural for you to feel indifference to your feelings, but indifference is not what heals. The shadows that dance across your mind are the unfelt emotions you have stuffed deep down inside you.

Learn to make friends with them, for they will lead you into a life with less strife. Unless, of course, you like being a victim, then you don't have to take responsibility for yourself. Here's another question to ask yourself, "Do I truly want to take responsibility for my own life?"

There will be strong feelings that come up for you. These can be scary. I cannot stress enough that you must recognize a Power greater than yourself that you believe will support you through all this messy work. Utilize it! It's part of the package of loving yourself!

Asking yourself these important questions isn't about accepting the first answer that comes across your mind. It's about sitting quietly and really, sincerely, asking the questions, feeling the words of the questions as you ask them. Then listening very, and I mean *very*, closely for the answers!

Your ego mind talks, talks and talks. It feeds you fear.

The ego chatters long and loud. The spirit listens and speaks in a soft stillness.

The longest journey we take is the one from our intellect to our heart. The truths of ourselves lives in our hearts, not in our heads!

If you find yourself alone or isolating from the world, well, it's not natural, although it may feel as if it is. As human beings, we need relationships with others to fill those places within us that we can't fill alone. Isolation may have worked throughout your childhood, like staying in your room by yourself to keep from being the center of someone else's negative attention. As an adult, being here on this earth, it's about building loving and respectful relationships with ourselves and others. I'm not saying it is easy, I'm just saying it's one of the most important reasons we are here!

- What does a loving relationship look like to you?
- Do you find relationships comforting?
- What do you bring to the table in your relationships with family, friends, work associates, children, and spouse?
- What do others bring to the table?

Your feelings are intuitive messages from Spirit. They are not right or wrong, good or bad; they are emotional warnings that you are out of harmony with your Self, (God, as you understand God). When you resist or deny your healing feelings, you are disconnected from your inner Self.

The Feeling Chart below was created by John Gray to help us understand the language of feelings. He was born in

Houston, Texas, in 1951. He is an author and marriage and family therapist. One of his most famous book's is *Men Are from Mars, Women Are From Venus*.

John explains that when we are stuck in negative emotions, we attract negative situations. We mirror our inner experience through our reality in life. When we don't allow ourselves to feel our undesirable feelings, we become blocked from creating the life we want because we become disconnected from our truth, which is to be happy, and to love and be loved.

This is a new language to us; one we must learn to heal. I found it very helpful in being able to put correct words to my emotions instead of cuss words.

First, look at the "Emotional Block" column at the far right, we'll use Indifference, then move all the way over to the left of the chart to "Healing Feeling," which is Sorrow.

Ok, I'm feeling Sorrow. Why am I feeling Sorrow? To get some insight, I move to the "Holistic Benefits" section of the chart, here I see that the reason my intuitive heart is sending me a "Sorrow" message is because I am feeling Grief. Now, I can look at the "General Feeling" column for more feeling information, which is the emotion of Powerlessness.

Using the Feeling Chart on page 39 to identify your emotions, write a feeling letter to a person who has left you with a negative feeling.

Recall a time you felt betrayed, then explore the four emotions of anger, sadness, fear, and sorrow, then write a feeling letter addressed to who you believe has left you feeling angry. The feeling of blame could be your emotional block.

Write your letter something like this:

Dear _____;

I feel betrayed that....
I am angry that...
I am sad that...

I am afraid that...
I am sorry that....
I want....

Don't send the letter to the person. It is only for your healing, not for changing someone else's behaviors. You are to stay on your own side of the road here. This is all about you!

I write letters to my Higher Power, which is Jesus, about negative feelings I experience. I do this because I believe my feelings and thoughts manifest in the physical world, and I desire to attract more positive experiences than negative ones. One tool I use to move through the discomfort of depression, anger, sadness, confusion, or frustration is to surrender to them in gratitude. You won't believe this at first, but when you allow yourself to feel icky feelings in gratitude, for they have a message of healing for you, you will feel much better, much faster than you dreamed possible!

A note here: I found that I had to learn how to feel positive feelings. One tool I use to do this is listening to music from recording artists such as Karen Drucker. Check her out on YouTube.

Our feelings are always changing, just like our thoughts. I like to think of them as stormy dark clouds darkening the sun, or billowing, marshmallow clouds floating across a sunlit blue sky.

> **"The first thing you have to know is yourself. A man who knows himself can step outside himself and watch his own reactions like an observer."**
> —Adam Smith, *The Money Game*

FEEL TO RELEASE CHART

Healing Feeling	Holistic Benefits	General Feeling	Emotional Block
39. Anger	Boundary Defense	Betrayal	Blame
40. Sadness	Endings	Abandonment	Depression
41. Fear	Warning	Uncertainty	Anxiety
42. Sorrow	Grief	Powerlessness	Indifference
43. Frustration	Persistence	Dissatisfaction	Judgment
44. Disappointment	Detachment	Discouragement	Indecision
45. Worry	Preparation	Helplessness	Procrastination
46. Embarrassment	Self-Acceptance	Inadequacy	Perfectionism
47. Envy	Motivation to Change	Deprivation	Resentment/Jealousy
48. Hurt	Self-Awareness	Exclusion	Self-Pity
49. Scared	Beginnings	Hopelessness	Confusion
50. Shame	Remorse	Unworthiness	Guilt

The language of feelings is not an exact science.

Make copies of this chart and place it in every room in your home, so that when feelings come up that draw your attention, you have this chart handy to help you learn the language of feelings. Learn to make friends with your feelings and intuition because they ARE your friends.

13
KNOWLEDGE OF YOUR TRIBE

YOU MAY FIND that the word "tribe" will help you understand the deep connection you have with your family. All tribes have beliefs that are passed on to the next generation, through attitudes, assumptions, and actions.

To change your consciousness, thinking in new and higher levels of awareness is work that is done in the secret place of your imagination and prayer closet.

Warning!

Outside of yourself, your tribe is the next most powerful force of resistance you will have to work with when you are determined to change your belief systems. You will be challenged. You may be asked, "Why are you doing this to me?" You must be very strong to break the cycle of generational abuse!

A spiritual law of inner change is not to talk about it with others. When you go around blabbing your desires and ambitions, you are siphoning off the energy of the desire, which weakens your commitment to yourself. Secondly, others will echo your present fears.

It is best to keep it a secret between yourself and your Higher Power and a very good counselor who can help guide you through the stages of awareness until you feel strong enough to walk through the challenges you will face with your tribe. Believe me, there will be confrontations!

When you make the decision to change how you view yourself, your family and friends will become afraid. They will know you are changing because of new ways you respond in your relationship with them. They may attempt to stop you from changing by making you feel guilty or ashamed. This is natural. It's mis-guided love.

Let's begin with these questions to ask in your journal, "What are some of the stories I was told about my grandparents?"

Sit quietly and picture yourself talking with family members; see if you can remember any stories you were told about your parents' lives when they were growing up. Can you remember family gatherings? What took place during these times that stick out in your memory?

For instance, one of my memories is mother making homemade eggnog. It had to be around Christmas time because that's when folks usually drink eggnog, right? I was almost three years old. We were standing next to the kitchen counter, where the big mixing machine was making a very loud noise. Mom was pouring an amber colored liquid from a large, long-necked bottle into the turning bowl of eggnog. She looked down at me and asked if I would like a taste. Of course, I would. I will never forget that I knew in that moment I was tasting eggnog with alcohol and black pepper in it.

Is this memory a valid one? Yes, most of the adults in my life before I was five years old were practicing alcoholics.

This is how to begin to unravel the mysteries of yourself. As you go back to gather data, along the way, if you are willing, you will begin to feel your emotions of events that took place, instead of intellectualizing them. Eventually, "feeling" will add color and dimension to your memories, allowing the emotions to rise and pass through you. Even the very scary ones will bring relief and healing.

Here is a meditation to allow stuck emotions to come up and pass through you. You may want to play instrumental meditation music in the background.

Sit in a comfortable chair, with your feet on the floor, your arms resting at your sides with your palms open and facing up. Close your eyes and breathe deeply in through your nose to the count of seven, hold your breath to the count of seven, then exhale to the count of seven. Notice how your breath feels when you inhale and how it feels when you exhale.

Now that your body is relaxed, focus on the emotion. Don't try to name it, simply feel it. Keep breathing in and out deeply, as this helps to move the stuck emotions out of you. You might only be able to do this for a few moments, but it's a beginning. Keep working with your breathing and emotions this way, and eventually you will feel a release.

When you allow your heart to truly feel your emotions, sometimes this can be frightening, because it can physically hurt. It hurts because you have locked the feelings deep inside you for fear of what they would do to your life if you let them come to the surface and get to know them. Your feelings will tell you the truth about what happened to you.

There are only two emotions we have, love and fear. Words like anger, sadness, and grief are all valid emotions, but they are just other words for "fear."

Please, I ask you to do your best not to judge your parents and other family members for what they did, as this will be extremely challenging in the beginning of your healing. Judging makes it a much more difficult road to travel to wholeness. Be willing to tell yourself, "They knew not what they were doing." Aren't you doing the best you can, and still make decisions that when acted upon you discover were not for the common good of all, including yourself? Have there not been times when you asked yourself, "Why did I not know what I was doing?"

When you put the pieces together about your parents' background, you may be surprised they did as well as they did. Possibly, your parents had such an abusive childhood, it's a wonder they came through it alive. They, just like you and me, created defenses and offenses to survive it. Our purpose is to discover what we were taught that doesn't serve our lives today!

Ask each question and wait for the answer before moving on to the next one.

Have you felt an unwarranted loyalty, not just with family, but also in other relationships as well, that may include work associates and friends?

Even though you didn't know what "boundaries" were in childhood, they were there. Somehow you knew they were not being respected; a creepy feeling may have come over you, what was happening in that moment just didn't "feel" right. You were a child, you couldn't put it into words, and you couldn't protect yourself, you may have believed you were being loved.

As an adult, you may not know how to protect yourself from what is taking place. It could be an inappropriate touch, it could be an aggressive attitude, such as being bullied, or an attitude of indifference, possibly paralyzing criticism, and/or physical abuse of family and friends.

Yet, when this happens, are you still a loyal friend, mate, or work associate?

Adult children who have been exploited by other adults, family members and/or non-family members, on a continuous basis, usually are loyal to folks that truly do not deserve their loyalty. We learn a distorted view of loyalty to others, as well as for ourselves.

Children conditioned in an abusive home, in adulthood often have a difficult time setting boundaries with others.

Often, we sell ourselves short because underneath the surface we are afraid of being hurt again, and usually will do just about anything not to feel alone and to be approved of by others.

Give yourself permission right here and now to be loyal to yourself; there is no one else who can do that for you. It's loving yourself!

Saying "no" to someone is a new way of saying "yes" to you.

Author Marianne Williamson says that sometimes we have to say "no."

"Sometimes we have to shut the door.

"Sometimes we have to lock the door.

"Sometimes we have to take away the key.

"And sometimes we have to call an attorney."

Even though you have autonomy, you are still a creation of your mother and father. In the womb, you were provided DNA and some of your parent's memories, as well as your ancestors and the conditioning experience of the environment they provided for you through the out-picturing of their beliefs and attitudes about themselves.

Research your tribe. A wealth of knowledge is waiting for you to help untether your consciousness of self-defeating beliefs!

Leave no stone unturned in this adventure. This is about you learning to be who you want to be.

14
THE ORPHANAGE

POINTING ABOVE MY head, the lady is telling me, "Kathy, this is your locker. Everything you own in the world will be put into this locker. These are your clothes."

They don't look like my clothes.

She continues, "And the drawer underneath this locker," she says as she opens it, "This is yours."

I see the white insides of the empty drawer.

The lockers are shiny dark wood.

They go to the ceiling!

How am I supposed to reach up there?

I don't ask the question.

She's tall, too!

She's saying something about this is my home now ....

In this hall of wooden compartments, the sun splashes through a big window. The dark brown cabinets radiate a glowing tunnel of mystical soldiers standing watch over me and the locker room.

I look past her into a tiled black and white checkered bathroom.

I'm lost ....
I feel twisted up inside ....
I hear our steps echoing off the shiny floor with blue swirls in it. We pass by rows of doors as we walk the long hall to my new bedroom.

She leads me into a room on the left at the end of the hall. There are four beds in it.

We stop at the bed on the left. It sits under large, long windows across the wall. She tells me, "Kathy, this is where you'll sleep. None of the beds have pillows, we can't afford pillows right now. Girls sleep at this end of the hall; the boys sleep at the other end of the hall."

She continues, "Girls are not allowed at the boys' end of the hall and boys are not allowed at the girls' end of the hall."

My sisters and brother aren't with me anymore.

The tall lady is telling me I am in an orphanage; this is where I live now!

She leaves me in the room, standing by the unfamiliar bed, beneath the windows, watching the leafy tops of trees float against the light blue sky.

Tears run out of my eyes.

I lay down on the bed without a pillow.

Did I do something bad to be here?

I curl up, wringing the white bedspread around me.

I twist and turn in agony as terror roars through my almost five-year-old body!

I cry out, "Daddy, where are you? I'm here. Come and get me!"

No one comes.

"Daddy, I'm afraid!"

No one hears me.

My face is hot and sticky, and it hurts.

I can't breathe through my nose.

When I awake from the exhaustion of crying, I hear children talking, laughing, and playing.

Dizzy, I stand up on my bed and look out the window and see a playground full of kids having fun!

There are huge trees, a swimming pool, swings, and a slide!

I sit with other kids at one of the round tables in the dining hall, eating my now favorite breakfast: oatmeal with butter, brown sugar, and milk.

I am learning how to ride a bike and swim here.

In the fall, we go for hikes to the apple trees. We pick baskets of apples and carry them back to the residential home to give to the person in the kitchen.

I don't know if I went to school before I came here to live. Sometimes I walk to school and back home again alone. I like the way our teacher has us sit in wooden chairs around her while she reads to us.

Grandma, the woman who comes at night, is skinny and she smiles a lot. She gives us Tootsie Roll Pops sometimes when we get into our beds. Grandma is nice to us; it feels like she loves us.

There isn't a daddy beating up a mommy here.

Sometimes I get to leave the orphanage and stay with families, in their home.

Sometimes I get to stay a while with a mean mommy.

Occasionally I get to go home with a nice mommy. She has dark hair and smells good. She made me a poodle skirt, but she won't let me take it back to the children's home. She has a sewing room. She puts the poodle skirt on me and white socks, then I run and slide down the hall with the shiny wooden floors in my white socks and black poodle skirt!

Then she didn't come to get me anymore.

I must have been bad.

She doesn't want me, either.

I miss her.

We kids talk among ourselves about finding a home and belonging to a family again. It's lonely in this hostel.

I felt like I was up on an auction block every time someone wanted to take me home for a weekend and test-trial me out, to see if I fit and if I didn't work out for them at least I had the "home" to return to.

No one sat down with me and explained what was happening when these folks would take me home for a few weekends and then I wouldn't see them again. I wasn't told I was worthy or valuable. I liken it to being cattle, horses, or swine on an auction block; no one cares about what the animal is feeling, they only want to know if their purchase is going to provide them with what they want.

I had a rage seizure in the locker room. Once again, I was being held down on the floor by the employees and went into a blackout.

At Christmas time, there was a huge, decorated pine tree in the living room of the children's home. It was a special time for us because the Big Sisters and Brothers would come and play with us. There was laughing and joy, like a real family on this holiday. Yet, there was a gnawing inside me. I missed my "real" family.

The three years I was there, I had the mumps and chicken pox. For a while, I was put in a room that was all white. When I had the chicken pox, I was bathed and slathered in a pink lotion to help stop the itching and later placed in a dorm with many beds with other children. I would cry because I was sternly told not to scratch where I itched because it would leave scars on my skin.

I felt tremendous fear and extremely alone during this time. There was not a mommy soothing me, there was only staff, too busy to offer much-needed emotional support during these illnesses.

Even among all the children with me and proficient personnel in the orphanage, I intuitively knew I was on my own.

"An orphan is not weak, because reality makes them stronger than a beast."
—Remon Rakibul

15
THE HISTORY OF AMERICAN ORPHANAGES

INSTITUTIONALIZED CHILDREN ARE not emotionally supported by staff. We are not held on anyone's lap, no one kisses the boo-boo's away. We aren't cuddled up with a caring adult just before falling asleep, being read bedtime stories. Our basic needs were met: shelter, food, clothing, playtime, and education.

When the night attendant would leave our room after bed check, sometimes we'd share beds together, holding and touching each other. Intuitively, we knew we needed this little bit of affection to survive the emotional coldness of residential care.

The earliest forms of orphanages were created in the 1700's. They became more organized establishments in the 1800's because of the explosion of immigrants arriving in the United States. Many children lost their parents to epidemics; others were surrendered by families living in poverty or struggling with drug or alcohol addiction.

Traditional orphanages in the United States began closing following World War II, as public social services were on the rise. U.S. adoption policy and procedures, as well as child-protection laws, began to take shape, leading to the demise of traditional American orphanages, which were replaced with individual and small-group foster homes.

A progressive movement of reformers, rethinking American orphanage systems, began in the early 1900's, thus the earliest child-welfare system was born.

President Theodore Roosevelt led this change by joining with leading childcare experts of the time. These leaders had a vision for child welfare, forming the United States Children's Bureau.

At that time, current economic growth in the U.S. enabled parents not only to care for their own children, but also open their homes to foster abandoned children. As a result of the efforts of Teddy Roosevelt and his conference of out-of-the-box child-welfare thinkers, today foster care is the most common form of support for children to be adopted or reunited with their families.

In the early spring of 1995, Minnesota's Family and Children's Services Division created a report of the effects of institutional care on children, which echoed my experiences of utilitarian care.

They discovered orphanages were in direct contrast to human nature, the essential innate sense of freedom, which is what children are supposed to be learning and doing. Institutions demand order, precision, form and conformity concerning all matters of life, there is no room for change or individualism, which naturally requires considerable discipline for the preservation of its rules.

Because of this required rigidness of institutional conditioning, children, me included, become impaired of the inability to bond. Bonding with others came much later in my life, yet still today to bond with others, except my daughter, is difficult. Along with this challenge, the ability to problem-solve is emotionally taxing, making it tough to turn to others for help, which leads to poor peer relationships, disciplinary problems, and naturally disruptive behaviors.

Children, like myself, who lived for very long periods of time in an institutional setting feel uncomfortable, not supported or looked-after, unloved, untrusted, untrusting and unwanted.

These children suffer from the unacknowledged grief and anguish of abuse, abandonment, or neglect. An institutional system cannot handle these children's emotional needs or provide them with the necessary counseling and services needed to help them begin to heal at an early age.

My experiences as a child living long term in institutional care has left its marks on me for life. I lack the ability to sustain long-term intimate relationships. I have no problem walking away from people or situations that are uncomfortable for me, even if it's advantageous for me to stay. I am quite content to be alone most of the time and find when I am with the same folks for more than a few days at a time, I become irritable and want to take flight. Yet, my close friends, as well as my daughter, all can bond with others and developed close, long-term intimate relationships. I do not have the patience for it because it feels suffocating.

I was one of those children who was placed in different foster homes without much nurturing. For these foster parents, it is all about the money they received from the state at the time to take in foster children. Today, adults considering child foster care have to undergo rigid compliances to become eligible to take a child in their home.

My siblings and I were children of parents who lost their parental rights. We became wards of the state because of the severity of home life with our parents.

I was one of those children who had numerous placement failures; back then I was told it was because I was an older child. My siblings were not institutionalized, they were placed in homes right away. I was not considered a suitable candidate for adoption. I was one of those children in our society who needed the most care and support. I felt, as a child, that the folks who adopted me thought that I should be so grateful to them for making me a distant part of their family.

Right after I was adopted in 1960, orphanages were becoming almost extinct.

There are still a few around, considered to be "residential treatment centers." The Village of Boys Town, which Father Edward Flanagan created as a self-governing system in 1926 for its citizens to build character, citizenship, and sense of community, was one of the evolved institutions that were stable living environments to meet the emotional and psychological needs of children in residential care.

When I stayed with a family for a weekend and they gave me fruit and candy upon returning to the children's home, I would gather my friends behind the gigantic tree, beside the swimming pool, and share my loot! It was so much fun to eat the treats with other kids. I pretended I was with my sisters and brother.

> **"Orphanages are the only places that ever left me feeling empty and full at the same time."**
> —John M. Simmons

16
ENTOMBED

Hurling in space.

Unknown companions.

Shadow of souls and absent a face.

Jackals sit guard this misty, dark night;

Waiting for prey to take their flight.

Hollow laughter.

A treacherous sound.

Lurking 'round corners;

The haunted found.

17
A CHILD IS BORN!

I WAS MARRIED at sixteen years old to a man almost seven years older than I. Gary was a drug addict at the time, but I didn't know this. I was too young to consider that possibility and too naïve to be aware of signs of addiction. He didn't hit me, he didn't abuse me verbally, but he just wasn't available. Which makes perfect sense to me now, because I was used to indifference and being ignored, and not having my emotional needs met. But I was not conscious of these needs and desires at age sixteen. I just wanted my own family.

I dropped out of high school in the tenth grade to get married. I wasn't pregnant.

I had our child about two years into our marriage. My husband wasn't with me at the hospital, he was home sleeping. Gary worked and slept. I took care of everything else by myself.

I nursed my daughter the first six months of her life. When she was born, we both had complications and had to stay in the hospital for a week.

I was like any other new mother; I would wake up in the middle of the night and check on her to make sure she was all right. The truth is, I was making sure she was still alive. One night I was checking on her, standing over her crib, feeling content, when my mind flashed to a place that was an oscillating, multi-colored tunnel. I felt an urge to hurt my baby! It was strong. I heard screams and saw my head being slammed against a crib railing. There was a bright light that was dimmed by a smoky fog and I saw myself being sexually touched in my own crib by a woman, with a man standing beside her. I was frightened out of my mind that I could have such thoughts and feelings with my own child. I didn't know then the extent of abuse I had suffered as an infant and toddler at my own mother's hands.

I decided right then and there that I had to protect my baby girl from me! That decision went way down deep inside me and became a conviction that I built into my relationship with my child for many years.

For a long while I was indifferent to Devona, my daughter, because if I allowed myself to get too close, I might hurt her. Yet, somehow, through those years, my baby and I became very close. Obviously, I did something right.

In the process of Gary, (Devona's father), and I divorcing, I met a man, Rick. I was attracted to him to because he paid attention to me, never mind that he beat me a few times in front of my kid. When our divorce was final, Rick and I began living together. Devona was five years old. My child became lethargic and would fall asleep while eating her meals. I took her and myself to a counselor to see what was going on. We were interviewed separately.

After the interview, this insightful counselor explained to me that Devona was having an identity crisis and needed to be with her father. I finally admitted to myself that my five-year-old daughter was very wise and had made up her mind that if I, her mother, couldn't see what was going on in the dangerous relationship between Rick and I, she was getting out of there! Her father is a peaceful man. Rick was someone to be very afraid of.

    I felt frightened for her because I knew her father worked long hours and slept a lot. Also, I felt devastated with fear that my worst nightmare had come true, I was a horrible mother!
    The counselor explained to me that I could make her stay with me, but that would be selfish of me, which was true. I had to consider her welfare over mine. I let her go.
    Her dad and I lived only a few miles apart, so for five years I was the parent who picked up the child every other weekend. Let me tell you, back in the 1970's that was not something a mother did. The thing was if there was a divorce and there were children involved, the woman took everything she could from her ex-husband, including the kids. I got flak from all sides. Yes, it bothered me, but my daughter's emotional health was far more important to me than what others had to say about how I was going about it to make sure she had what she needed, which was her father at that time.
    When she was with him, I worked full time and drank a lot. I was angry with myself and depressed.
    However, I did a lot of fun things with her while she was growing up. I would read to her, she really liked that. I would have her stay in the kitchen with me sometimes while I cooked so that she could learn how to cook herself. She is a wonderful cook today. We did crafts together and went for walks together.
    I must be honest here; unknowingly at the time, I suffered from Post Traumatic Disorder, causing memory lapses for me. Consequently, there are some wonderful memories Devona has shared with of stuff we did together when she was a kid that brought her happiness, that regretfully, I have no memory of. From my skewed vantage point at the time, I assumed that Devona's childhood was pain filled. She has told me several

times throughout her adulthood that she felt she had a much happier childhood than most her friends did.

She came to live with me full time when she was ten, going into the sixth grade. We lived in the country, on a farm. She loved it there. Her dad lived in the city. She raised hogs for the 4H Club she and I belonged to and won reserve grand champion and champion of home grown. Now she has the picture hanging on her office wall.

I was becoming sicker and sicker. I would be all right one moment and the next I would be screaming at her. I verbally abused my only child.

When she was fourteen, I was diagnosed with bipolar disorder. Six months later I seriously attempted suicide. When I woke up in the hospital, she was lying in the bed beside me, holding on to me. Once again, I made a decision that no matter how I felt about my life and life in general, no matter how much my sick brain told me to kill myself, I would not do that. I had her to think about. When I saw what I had done to her by trying to take my own life, I knew that I could not, under any circumstances, leave my baby with the legacy of me killing myself. The trauma of that would have devastated her.

In many ways, my daughter was the mother and I was the child. Yet somehow, we remained very close.

I respected her boundaries. We could talk about anything. I was very protective of her. When she was seventeen, we were shopping, and I went into one of my tirades. She looked me square in the eyes and pronounced, "Mom, I don't have to take that from you anymore!" I looked at her, amazed, and immediately stopped talking like that to her for thirty-some years now.

Six months of seeing a psychiatrist and being told that if I didn't change the way I lived I was going to die a violent death, (this was after the suicide attempt) I looked inside myself and knew he was right. My family of origin was violent. My father had guns all over his house. My half-sister carried a gun and my sister Vicki lived a violent life, receiving beatings from her boyfriends and causing many problems in the family with her angry attitudes. Linda, my younger sister, killed herself using a gun with the help of a boyfriend, leaving behind her four-year-old daughter to be raised by a father who was seriously and openly addicted to pornography. I was the quieter version of violence among my family members. I would be internally violent with myself.

In 1985 I decided to move to Colorado to receive a more advanced treatment for my issues. I had two U-hauls packed with our things and was ready to leave the next morning when Devona came to me saying she didn't want to go with me, that her dad needed her more than I did. She was fourteen; she had the right to choose who she wanted to live with. Once again, we were separated. The next morning on the way out of Michigan, I dropped her and one of the U-hauls with her things in it off at her dad's.

I did find the help I needed in Colorado: a great counselor who understood what I wanted and needed for my life to change into what I desired it to be. He put me into incest counseling, that's when I discovered that night long ago when my kid was an infant and I had the nightmare flashback of the tunnel, that I had been sexually abused. I was told I couldn't have made that up, because children don't have thoughts like that unless someone did something to them. The incest counselor asked me if I had ever abused my daughter sexually; no, I had not. She said that was very unusual, especially since my mother was the abuser. She told me I must be very strong not to act on my inclinations to be sexually abusive to my child. I didn't realize then what a big deal it was that I never touched her inappropriately. I didn't beat her. I didn't abandon her to strangers. She never was in the foster-care system or an orphanage.

With Devona living in one state and me living in another, I made sure she had graduation announcements.

Her grandmother, my adopted mother, made her graduation cake. We had her graduation party at her dad and Sandy's home. She knew her education was very important to me. She saw me go back to night school when she was seven to acquire my diploma, while I worked sixty hours a week as an assistant manager of a fast-food restaurant.

Later we went through massage school together and while she was attaining her education to become a licensed cosmetologist, I attended the same school to become a licensed esthetician.

Trust me, I paid for screaming at her when she was in her early thirties. She punished me for quite some time. I took it because I knew she needed to do that to get it out of her system. I knew I deserved for her to be very angry with me. It was safe for her then, because I had come back from Colorado a changed person in many ways. When I finally had enough of being her whipping post for the past, I stood up to her one day. Devona apologized and I said, "It's okay, this gave me an opportunity to practice not being a codependent to you."

I learned to apologize to my kid for the things I had done that caused her anguish as a child. Even today, if something comes up for her that she needs to say to me about her childhood experiences, we talk and if I feel I need to say, "I'm sorry I hurt you," I do.

I believe with all my heart that one of the biggest gifts we can give our adult children is to listen to their interpretation of our behaviors when they were growing up and sincerely apologize to them for the stuff we did unconsciously that hurt them. It's important that we forgive ourselves, also. We knew not what we were doing. We only did what we were taught to do as parents from our parents. I was screamed at, beaten and molested, along with all the other shit that went on. I didn't come close to doing to my daughter what was done to me. The thing that stayed with me was being screamed at all the time in the adopted family. I could have told you some fairy-tale story about the relationship between my daughter and me, but you would have known I was lying. One of the most important aspects of writing this book is for me to be authentic with you.

Today, Devona is comfortably married; she waited until she was in her late forties before she made that commitment. She works her dream job from her beautiful home, bringing in a substantial five-figure income. I love my son-in-law; he treats her very well. He often tells me he loves me.

Devona and I have never parted all through her life without saying, "I love you," and hugging.

Raising her, I was full of turmoil most of the time, not because of her, but because there were tapes playing in the background of my unconscious mind. I had suppressed most of the realities of my childhood to survive it and to survive being a mother and adult.

One thing I know for sure, a Power greater than myself was with us during those years, because we have maintained a close relationship through all of it. She didn't become an addict or spend time in prison or choose to live the gang life. She's had both her biological parents all her life.

She is my testament to breaking the cycles of generational abuse. I wouldn't have been able to do it without her by my side.

18
BOUNDARIES

> "Every time I have to set a boundary, it stresses me out. But I do it for the same reason I built blanket forts when I was a little kid. To create a safe place for myself."
> —Unknown

BOUNDARIES ARE NECESSARY for your inner and outer safety. Adults with abusive childhoods have a difficult time discovering what their boundaries are. You have boundaries, but often they're buried under the unrelenting demands of survival from manipulation, neglect, and exploitation.

For the first seven-and-a-half years of my life, I was in various environments with different belief systems, and of course everyone had their own opinions about how, what, and who I needed to be to be accepted by them. Whew! It was enormously taxing.

Growing into adulthood, being married, I didn't know anything about who I was. I was to be what someone else thought I should be, to please them. People could say and do just about anything with me. I was not taught that I was worthy or that I had power of any kind. A friend once told me that I didn't appear to have an ego; that I lacked a personal identity.

As a child, I became enmeshed with the power figures who heaped upon me their versions of who and what I was supposed to be.

Where do the people outside you end, and you begin?

Wikipedia's definition of boundaries: "Personal boundaries are guidelines, rules, or limits that a person creates to identify reasonable, safe, and permissible ways for other people to behave toward them and how they will respond when someone passes those limits."

Our boundaries begin to form while we are still infants. If we are born into a nurturing family, it becomes safe for us to become individuals, to be different from other family members.

A father might have baby monitors in his children's play areas to listen to their conversations with each other. If they say something that threatens his authority and he feels they are being disloyal to him, he punishes them. He is teaching his children they are not allowed to have or to express their individual feelings, opinions, or a right to privacy. They are being conditioned in codependency, enmeshment, lack of self-sufficiency; they are hostages; therefore, they lack the freedom of autonomy from other members of their family unit. This parent's rules teach his children they are not sovereign, they are not allowed to develop self-direction and self-governing boundaries. He is training his kids that they are extensions of their father. His children must think, feel, and believe what he thinks, feels, and believes. They are there to serve him. He is denying his children their self-identity! This is boundary violation.

Boundaries are not all the same. It depends on who you're interacting with that determines if the boundary is flexible or not.

When you are in the company of someone who is consistently refusing to accept "no" as the answer to the same question, know that if you continue a friendship with that person, they will constantly be challenging your boundaries. In some ways, it's like a game for him or her. Usually this is happening on an unconscious level, to see how much of yourself you are willing to give away for them. When folks behave this way, it's an indication they were raised in an environment that devalued their boundaries.

Frequently, knowing your boundaries or not, you intuit when someone is misrepresenting themselves or lying to you. This not only takes place in personal relationships but professional ones as well. Most of the time we may have to put up with being lied to in the work arena. In personal relationships, we can set boundaries more freely and we don't have to accept someone else's behavior if we feel violated.

Creating healthy boundaries, which allows others to know whether they can go there or not with you, is another way of loving others as well as loving yourself.

Saying "no" to what others expect from you, inappropriate touching, criticism, verbal abuse, indifference, making comments about your body that make you feel uncomfortable, is truly saying "yes" to yourself. This concept can be upsetting when you first put it into action, because you don't feel comfortable setting boundaries yet. Try it, see how you feel about saying "no" to someone or something you really don't want to interact with. It may be a little scary at first, but as you "practice" setting your boundaries, you will begin to build self-confidence.

I cannot stress to you enough that to create healthy boundaries, you must allow yourself to feel your feelings, not intellectualize them. How can you create boundaries if you don't know what and how you feel about yourself and the world around you?

To help you create healthy boundaries, I suggest that you read two books: Melody Beattie's, *Co Dependency No More* and Anne Kathrine's, *Boundaries-Where You End, and I Begin.* These two books are a great place to begin healing enmeshment and codependency, which is being controlled by and becoming an extension of another person. Getting to know your boundaries is a much-needed guide into discovering your authentic self, therefore, allowing others to know the real you.

As a child, you didn't have the power to set boundaries. One of the most challenging truths I discovered about parents is they unconsciously manifest or project in their present life the attitudes, beliefs, and feelings they grew up with. If no one wakes up and smells the coffee, all of it gets passed down from one generation to the next. Please, remember what Abraham Lincoln had to say about mercy, especially when you are walking through memory lane to discover who you really be.

"I have always found that mercy bears richer fruits than strict justice."

Physical boundaries are choosing who can touch you, how and where you can be touched. Your emotional boundaries are set by choosing how you will let people treat you.

A woman I know, when she has directly communicated her boundary with someone and they continue to regard her in a manner she deems as inappropriate, then mirrors back their behavior. When she is asked, "Why are you treating me this way?" Her usual response is, "I've asked you not to treat me like this, but you continue this behavior. Apparently, you want me to treat you the same way you're treating me." Her explanation is the Golden Rule that says "Do unto others as you would have them do unto you." If a person doesn't respect her boundaries, they are telling her they don't respect themselves.

How do you get to know who you are? Through learning to feel your feelings, and trust your feelings, because your feelings never lie to you!

When you have loving protective boundaries in place, and can clearly communicate them to others, you create respectful and loving relationships. The folks in your life who don't respect your boundaries are indirectly telling you they don't really want to get to know you and sooner or later, you will feel that.

There are thousands of boundary messages you send through your interactions with others: your facial expression, a look in your eyes, moving closer or farther away from someone, smiling, frowning, having a poker face, verbally communicating exactly what your boundary is, and many, many more expressions of where others end, and you begin.

"It is necessary and even vital to set standards for your life and the people you allow in it."
—Mandy Hale

A woman told me an experience she had working for a retail company. She was required to wear a mask and was working in an enclosed glass area; it was eighty-five degrees outside that day. This woman communicated her physical boundaries, explaining to her manager there was no air flow in that area, she couldn't breathe, and she was not going to stand in there. He called her behavior "insubordinate" and ordered her to clock out for the day. He was indifferent toward her valid complaint. She told me that the next day there was a fan placed in her work area. It cost her a day's wages, but as we all know, freedom is not free, and that includes setting our boundaries!

A man told me his story of having problems with a woman he had dated. She wouldn't understand that he couldn't be with her every minute of the day and was continuously asking him to explain himself to her as to why he had to take care of his own business. He told me this woman would throw fits if he didn't do what she wanted him to do. She overlooked just about everything that was important to him, turning most of the conversations into what she wanted and needed. She often attempted to use emotional blackmail to manipulate him. The reason I tell you this story is because this guy knows his boundaries! He stood his ground and eventually he told her, "No! Which part of no don't you understand, the "N" or the "O"? Don't call me again!" Saying "no" is a complete sentence. Sometimes you must get downright raw with others where your boundaries are concerned.

Boundary violations hurt and can stay with us for a lifetime, especially when they happen in childhood.

When I was a kid, I didn't like to eat eggs, especially runny ones. I was placed in a foster home where the woman there would literally force soft poached eggs down my throat! Consequently, I wouldn't eat eggs after that, and chose lunch or dinner foods for breakfast. I have worked through my feelings about this boundary violation, and today I can occasionally eat hard-cooked eggs for breakfast. Boundary violations can leave their mark on us for life.

It's important for you to learn your boundaries and limits and make friends with them. Maybe you haven't done this type of work before. When you do inner work, try looking at it this way; you are getting to know someone, the most important person you can know. You!

19
THE EFFECTS OF DOMESTIC VIOLENCE ON CHILDREN

THE EFFECTS OF witnessing the violence between your parents began when you were in the womb. When I began counseling for childhood issues, the doctor told me I responded to life as a child who had been in a war.

Professionals have discovered through infant brain imaging that while an infant is sleeping, or in the uterus, that exposure to domestic violence can reduce parts of the brain, change its overall structure, and the way the circuits work together.

Also, research has determined that children witnessing domestic violence are likely to have Post-Traumatic Stress Disorder, like soldiers returning from war.

Domestic violence feels scarier than war. When a fetus is in the womb and there is domestic violence taking place in the home, the unborn child's brain development takes a big hit. This is because it is witnessing and experiencing abuse. A child, in any stage of development who witnesses abuse, is a victim. We are supposed to feel safe with our parents, in the home they provided for us. As children, we are powerless over what we witness. When I was in counseling, I gained the knowledge, then the feelings, and then a full awareness, that I reacted to life as an adult like a child who had been in a war zone.

In the childhood conditioning in my natural parents' home and my adoptive parents' household, I believed for a long while that the way to handle life's problems was with emotional and verbal violence and in some cases, physical violence. I worked in a bar to support myself and Devona when her father and I separated. A few times I had to resort to physical violence to protect myself from other women who wanted to start a fight with me. I am not a big woman, but I was a hell cat when I felt pushed into physical violence. The other person always came out on the short end of the stick. In my distorted view, I felt this behavior made me powerful. I discovered, however, that I was making a jackass out of myself.

There were years I blamed the orphanage for not providing me with emotional support. I was quite pissed! I blamed God, too.

Eventually, I was able to see they didn't take me out of my home; that the orphanage was a place of refuge.

Even though I may not have conscious memories of the physical violence that took place in the home of my origins, I am aware of its effects on my brain chemistry, as well as my abilities to emotionally connect with myself and others. For instance, I don't have the natural mental and emotional filters most people do. Stress gets stuck in my physical body, so when this happens, I may experience temporal seizures. Therefore, I am selective about television programs I watch, movies I go to, music I listen to, books I read, and the company I keep.

Negative self-talk is no different than gossiping about someone; it hurts you and others, and it determines what your life experiences are going to be.

In the beginning of practicing monitoring my inner speech, I discovered violent punitive and cruel self-talk and felt the emotions arising from it, which caused feelings of guilt, shame, self-hatred, and separation from self, others, and God.

I again turned to the Bible to strengthen my faith and provide the courage I needed to evolve this destructive dialect into loving self-communication.

Deliver me not over unto the will of mine enemies: for false witnesses are risen up against me, and such as breathe out cruelty. I had fainted, unless I had believed to see the goodness of the Lord in the land of the living.
—Psalms 27:12-13

This is the verse I translated into referring to my enemies as being unloving self-talk and beliefs I was hypnotizing myself with.

Deliver me not unto the will of my thoughts and my feelings, for they speak out cruelty and are lies and false witnesses my ego uses to separate me from God. I had fainted, unless I believe to see the goodness, (love and mercy), of the Lord in the land of the living.

Love heals. Fear steals.

Ernest Holmes states, in his book, *Love and Law*, "We are hypnotized from cradle to death." It is extremely important for your well-being that you become aware of the foundation from which you speak to yourself. Is it a foundation of love, or one of fear? Teach yourself discernment of your thoughts. Choose carefully those with which you would hypnotize yourself.

Your thoughts create feelings, which give your thoughts power to create the reality you are living in now. Pay attention to your thoughts!

Learn to surrender in gratitude to experiences that most folks cannot relate to because of your unusual childhood encounters. These occurrences provide a deep inner-strength and wisdom that will come out of hiding when you focus on healing your inner world.

This is one more step in breaking generational abuse and abandonment.

20
ADOPTIVE PARENTS' BACKGROUND

MY ADOPTED FATHER John was raised in a Christian home with two brothers. His father was a preacher man from Missouri. When he was fifteen years old, he earned a living wrestling. His first marriage was to a woman who had a daughter. He caught her in bed with another man. And Dad was addicted to gambling.

In our family unit, he didn't interact with my adopted sister, Barb and I much. Once he took us to a drive-in to see *Lady and the Tramp*. In the winter he would clear the snow off the frozen lake we lived on so we could ice skate. He always wore a brimmed hat, sat in the living room in front of the television, eating his supper. He sat with the family for meals only when there was company. He enjoyed watching wrestling and occasionally would wrestle with my sister and me while he was watching one of these matches. He rarely talked with us. Dad and Mom displayed very little affection between them in front of us. He didn't go to church with us. He was like a ghost living in the house.

Dad was always tinkering with a vehicle or a small tractor in the garage when he wasn't working at the automotive plant.

His mother, Granny, lived with us; Mom appeared not to like her very much. She told us she felt that having his mother living with them was a hindrance to her marriage. As a kid, I couldn't understand this, because Granny grew a garden, canned its bounty, watched my sister and I while Mom worked and made sure there was dinner on the table every night for the family. Both my parents worked full-time jobs.

Mom was raised in Michigan. Her mother had been sick, and she witnessed her father push her mother down the stairs. Her mother died when Mom was about four years old. Mom had two sisters and a brother. (I also had two sisters and a brother).

My adopted mother began working at an early age cleaning houses. She developed tuberculosis in her early twenties and was in a sanatorium for almost two years. She was dating Dad before she became ill, so he was with her during this time of her life. Later, she worked for years as a bookkeeper and secretary for a real-estate company.

Mom and Dad's relationship appeared distant and cold. They didn't touch or kiss, rarely they would talk to each other in front of us. Yet dad and mom got up every morning at four a.m. This was the time of day they connected, while the rest of the family was sleeping. I woke up early one morning it was still dark outside, having to go to the bathroom. We had an open staircase, as I descending the steps, I saw them kissing and intimately touching each other. I was ten years old, at this point I had lived with them for almost three years. It was the first and the last time I saw a display of affection between them.

I lived with these folks for seven-and-a-half years. In that household, everything was a secret.

In my adopted family, Dad and Granny would whisper between themselves. Granny and Mom would whisper between themselves. Mom and my adopted sister would go off together, never inviting me along. I felt an expansive, hollow emptiness with them.

I felt a constant heavy atmosphere of separation and anger living in this household. Every now and then, my adopted Dad and sister "B," would get into a physical fight, sounding and moving like snarling dogs through the house. I would back into the nearest corner and freeze.

Granny would come into the room I was in after one of these explosions and growl, "Are you happy now?" As a kid, I never understood her anger with me. I was not a part of "that."

Then one day, about seven years into being with this family, Granny was working in her garden on a blistering hot day. She stumbled into the house and laid down on her bed, apparently having a heat stroke. Her bedroom was just off the living room where my sister and I were watching television. She asked Barb, my adopted sister, "If I give you a dollar will you get some wet, cool rags and put them on my head and feet?"

Barb screamed at her that she wasn't going to do that, jumped off the sofa and stomped out the door in a huff. I was fourteen years old and I couldn't and still can't today understand her reaction to Granny asking for help.

I quietly walked up to where Granny was lying and I said, "Granny, I will get the rags for you, tell me what to do."

She looked at me, then replied, "There's fifty-cents in that drawer I'll give you to get some cool rags for my head and feet."

I looked at the drawer across the room she was pointing to answering, "I don't want the money, just tell me what to do."

When I looked into her eyes, they had changed from peering at me to actually seeing me for the first time. I saw a light in them for me that had not been there before.

From that day on, until I left there, which was only a few years later, Granny treated me lovingly.

"The opposite of love is not hatred, but indifference."
—Elie Weisel

21
SIBLING SEPARATION

> "Your siblings are the only people in the world who know what it's like to have been brought up the way you were."
> —Unknown

SIBLING RELATIONSHIPS ARE the longest relationships we have. They have an enduring importance, because they are linked to the formation of our identity and can provide us with a sense of belonging.

I always thought about my family of origin. I wanted to be with them. I felt driven to find them. It didn't matter about the violence, abuse, or neglect that I witnessed back then; I had a sense of belonging to them that endured. The day at the State Police post, sitting by the pool with my brother and two sisters, was the last time we were together.

In my mind, heart, and soul I feel a disconnect from friends in my life that have deep and lasting relationships with their siblings.

Without my siblings, I felt I didn't have an identity; the loss of them left me with a lifelong feeling of not belonging. I suffered for years from Separation Anxiety Disorder, (SAD). This is a feeling of excessive unease and apprehension from being removed from the family to which I had a strong emotional attachment. This carried on into adulthood. Even today, if a biological family member gets in touch with me through social media, I will usually attempt to emotionally connect with them. Sometimes I can, but most of the time I cannot because they still live in the past and are unwilling to see life a little differently.

Definition of pathologically: When the intensity, duration, and/or frequency of anxiety become distressful and chronic, it interferes with a person›s functioning and well-being.

I experienced social anxiety for years. I felt very uncomfortable in public situations; even going shopping, anxiety would rear its head. Sometimes I would begin to cry, and even would have to go out into the parking lot and vomit because of crippling fear. When I would attend parties, I couldn't engage in conversation, would stay only for an hour and leave without saying good-bye to anyone. I reacted to life this way because I didn't feel I belonged … anywhere. Many times, I struggled with thoughts and feelings that I didn't have a right to breathe!

Have you had these kinds of experiences? Please, write about them; the writing will help you see more clearly how you may have been affected through the loss of siblings.

There was no one there, in the orphanage, the foster homes, or the family that adopted me, who spoke to me of my loss. In fact, I wasn't allowed to speak of it.

Even if you have never spoken to your children about these things, or talked in generalities with them about your childhood, children feel their parents' emotions. They know stuff about you that would surprise you! If you can't find the love you need for yourself to begin to heal, look into your child's eyes and heart, you will find it there. Allow it to provide you with the courage, bravery, strength, and motivation to change your self-beliefs. It will be one of the greatest gifts of love you can give them and yourself.

You may find that giving your child or children the love and attention you were denied in childhood may be just the medicine you need to heal your soul. What have you got to lose? You get to make choices today, it's up to you. Who do you want to be?

> **For to be free is not merely to cast off one's chains, but to live in a way that respects and enhances the freedom of others.**
> —Nelson Mandela

22
ARRIVAL INTO A NEW FAMILY

MRS. MC HAS been coming for a while every weekend to take me home with her.

She gives me candy, fruit, sometimes some pennies and nickels on Sunday evenings when she brings me back to the orphanage. I share the fruit and candy with my friends behind the big tree next to the swimming pool.

I don't recall being in her house on the "visiting" weekends, and I don't remember Mr. Mc, Granny and Sister being there. Childhood amnesia, maybe. Or maybe, all I could accept was there may be a new mommy for me.

Once, I remembered the long drive from her house back to the orphanage because there was a very bad car accident, police cars and ambulances. Two people were moving a table with wheels on it, and a bloody sheet covered a long lump on the table.

New mom gave me a stuffed, fluffy, pink and white Easter bunny, so I must have been with her on an Easter weekend. I took the bunny to school for show and tell.

Then one day I was told to pack my things. I was leaving the "home."

My meager belongings were packed into a small, round suitcase, placed on the sofa in the living room of the orphanage, with my pink, fluffy friend sitting on top of it. I have a home now because Mrs. Stratton, she was the manager of the orphanage, told me I was adopted!

My adopted mom, Mrs. Mc walks through the giant double doors to the living room! She's smiling, she's happy to see me! I have a mommy now!

I feel so happy!

We get my things, take them to her car; I am leaving the orphanage forever!

There's another girl in the car, in the front seat, I don't remember her before!

Mrs. Mc is explaining to me this is my new sister now, Barb.

Wow! I have a sister, too!

My new mom is explaining that we must stop by my new daddy's gas station and see him. I don't remember seeing him during my visits with Mrs. Mc — I mean mom.

As we step into the gas station, my nose is filled with the aroma of oil and rubber. There is my new daddy, and I'm told the other man is my new Uncle Bill.

New dad doesn't say anything to me, and neither does new uncle. They play, talk, and laugh with my new sister.

There is a machine with different colored gum balls inside it in front of the window. Sister demands some money for the machine.

No one offered me a nickel for the gumball machine. All four of them are standing together away from me, and not talking with me. In fact, they act like I'm not here. They're talking and playing with my new sister, Barb.

Suddenly, I feel something in my chest move, like something just broke.

I feel deep sadness.

I thought they wanted me. They adopted me, didn't they? Why are they acting like I'm invisible?

Something inside me stands up tall and straight and an inner voice, strong and firm speaks:

"You are not my family!"

Consequently, because of this experience compounded with emotional and physical abuse soon after I arrived into this family, I could not establish a deep emotional connection with them.

Soon after being adopted, I watched the *Wizard of Oz* movie upstairs, alone. It had a powerful effect on me as a child adjusting to a new family, and their attitude of indifference toward me.

In this context of magical thinking, I connected with the character, Dorothy, clicking her heels together, chanting, "There's no place like home." I felt I needed to search for my siblings and my "home" and the song, *Over the Rainbow* gave me the inspiration I needed to continue seeking out my "real" family. When I found them, it was a bizarre and gruesome awakening! It certainly wasn't the happy ending of *The Wizard of Oz!*

My sister, Vicki, had been back with our family of origin for a few years before I connected with them. She had been wreaking havoc all over the place. You know the story, emotionally blackmailing both our parents because she deserved to have them make up to her what was lost. She had an affair with one of our first cousins, which upset our father to no end. Everything dad tried to do for her to show her that he loved her and was remorseful for what happened, she puked back in his face. She was hostile, to say the least. She blamed everyone for her self-made miserable life. She taught her sons to steal from their grandfather by instilling hatred in them. She called Dad and me to rescue her from her boyfriend who was beating her. When we got there, the boyfriend beat my aging father and she stood there watching. It was a set-up. Vicki was violent with everyone in her life, including her children.

After the initial contact was made and in the early stages of my birth father, Teats and I developing a relationship, I discovered he was, well, afraid of what torments I may have had in store for him. I didn't have any. I just wanted to be with my Dad, and I wanted Devona to have a relationship with her grandfather. She was still a toddler when grandpa came into her life, and the three of us became very close.

My birth mother, Delores had another family of three kids she was raising with her husband. Mom and Damien, her husband, beat the two youngest kids regularly. When my half-sister, Theresa was twelve years old, which was in that first year I came back, Mom kicked her out of the house. I was shocked. I attempted to intervene on this girl's behalf, but Mom wouldn't listen.

One of my first cousins approached me for a sexual encounter.

My half-sister was raped. Theresa came to my father for help and support because there was none coming from our mother and her stepfather.

My father had guns planted all over his house. For god sakes, he lived in a small farming town. One night I came in late and I needed to talk with him. When I turned on the light, he was pointing a .357 at me. When he saw it was me, he yelled at me for scaring him. That was because he was frightened that he was about to kill his own kid.

My dad's brother, Jimmy was in a mental institution. He was diagnosed with schizophrenia and had attempted to rape a woman. He was very creepy to be around at family gatherings.

And finally, the most gruesome of all, my baby sister Linda was living with a guy who was into porn and drugs. She was also dating another man who provided her with a .357 magnum and one day showed her how to kill herself with it in his living room. She left behind a four-year-old daughter to be raised by the porn junkie.

You know what I find very strange about all this, is that I was not deterred from wanting to be with my family of origin. I was raised by my adopted family in violent silence. In some ways all this seemed natural and normal to me.

For years I was ashamed because of where I came from. Not anymore. I have accepted it. My daughter and I were the only ones who made it out of there.

Vicki still lives the same life, mooching off folks and living out all her paranoid thinking, spilling it over on her two oldest sons. She convinced the younger of her sons that I killed his father, whom I had only met once, the night he beat my father. My nephew's father was murdered by the gang he and Vicki hung out with.

My intention is to help you understand that you are not alone, and you are not a freak. I tell you these things because my hope is to help you gather information that may help yourself or a loved one discover a mindful, self-loving path. Abused children endure emotional and psychological pain and are expected to keep going and smiling as if nothing is happening almost every day of their lives. This kind of torture would bring an adult to their knees begging for mercy.

You have survived physical, emotional, and spiritual abuse, and you kept going, hiding it away deep inside you. I beg you to take a deep look inside, especially if you have children of your own, become cognizant of them, interested in them, and responsive to their needs and their love for you as their parent.

> **"A child who is being abused by its parents doesn't stop loving its parents. It stops loving itself."**
> —Shahida Arabi

23
HOUSE ON THE LAKE

The house on the lake is now my leave to take.

The dam and Wilcox Mill; memories are clear still.

A house looking serene; inside horrors make up the scene.

Tall pines, fallen soft needles for making camps;

Willows weeping shadows across yard lamps.

On a peninsula the house sits; seemingly away from the world, in a pit.

There were lots of sunshiny days; in the house, the story unfolds of unkind ways.

Shouting and silence at the same time; the family, a family of mimes.

We swam and of hikes partook; catching turtles and frogs from murky brooks.

Still, there's hauntings from childhood ghosts;
being reduced to the fears and tears they host.

Granny teaching me how to fish; for supper eating
the delicate dish.

Inside the heart there ached to be a home, a haven,
safety for me.

Roasting mallows and dogs over a yard's work well done;
occasionally burning the fingers and thumb.

Inside the house, the truth well hidden,
understanding and compassion forbidden.

Loneliness, how it engulfed; staying in that room,
turning pain off.

Memories of Grandma visiting a while,
will always bring to my lips a smile.

The sun shines brightly over the house still; but inside,
no love, only lies and loneliness tilled.

24
MAGICAL THINKING

> One of the most tragic things I know about human nature is that all of us tend to put off living. We are all dreaming of some magical rose garden over the horizon instead of enjoying the roses that are blooming outside our windows today.
> —Dale Carnegie

SOMETIMES WE NEED fantasy to survive reality.

Children naturally believe there is a Source greater than themselves that provides them with magical powers. My experience in that first morning I awoke "alive" in my bed, I knew I was a spirit from heaven now living inside a human body. When I jumped down on the floor to run and tell my mommy I was alive that day, what I was confirming is that "I AM," my first awareness of consciousness!

Magical thinking is prominent in a child between the ages of two and seven. I was almost five years old when I believed magical thinking would save my family. I created a magical inner being that could transcend the viciousness of the environment I experienced.

Magical thinking is how children play and create a world. When we build sandcastles on a sun-drenched beach, we are creating a domain in which we have power. As children, magical belief is fuel for imaginary role-play and fantasizing that helps us cope with chaos and master difficult problems in life. It helps us as young children to maintain the feeling of independence and power, which is what kids mostly lack in real life.

Susan A. Miller Ed.D., Ellen Booth Church, and Carla Poole, pre-school educators, discovered in their research this about children and magical thinking:

Years 0-2
- Babies need to be the center of a loving, predictable world which is their essential core experience for all kinds of thinking, both magical and rational.

- Toddlers base their thinking on what they see, hear, and feel, often resulting in inaccurate but creative conclusions.

- Two-year-old's work hard, through much exploration, at developing their unique theories about the world.

Years 3-4
- Threes and fours often use magical thinking to explain causes of events.

- Preschoolers sometimes assign their own thinking as a reason for occurrences that are out of their control.

- Threes and fours believe, with their power of magical thinking, that they can change reality into anything they wish. Also, they believe that what they wish for or expect can affect what is really happening because of the preschooler's inclination toward magical thinking.

Years 5-6
- Fives and sixes move in and out of magical thinking as explanations for what they see.

Kindergartners use dramatic play to sort through what is fantasy and what is reality, thinking that inanimate objects can still come alive. Five and six-year-olds are still in an animistic stage. They give attribution of a soul to plants, inanimate objects, and natural phenomena. Children have a belief in a supernatural power that organizes and animates the material world. They also have a belief in spiritual beings.

Do you feel a deep responsibility, infused with entrenching guilt and shame because you couldn't do anything to stop the mistreatments you may have witnessed between your parents, and were inflicted upon your siblings and yourself?

Do you believe that you "caused" the perpetrator to act out?

Demoralized children are taught they are responsible for the cruelty inflicted upon them, and magical thinking is the tool they use to keep them somewhat sane and even possibly alive. When I witnessed father beating mother, for years I felt responsible because I couldn't protect her. In fact, my dad included me in his act of violence by demanding that I open the front door for him to kick my naked and bleeding mother through the screen door.

Ask yourself, "Did an adult in my childhood demand that I participate in the abuse of another?" If this has happened to you, self-compassion is essential not only for your adult self, but also for your inner child, who was without power. Often, children carry anger and even rage into adulthood because they feel responsible and couldn't do anything to protect themselves and others from the abuse.

An emotion that was in my subconscious mind for a long time was "defeat." When the dark car came that day, I discovered I wasn't strong, and I wasn't magical. It was all a dream.

Living in domestic violence, did you sense an unspoken conspiracy of silence?

Children experiencing fear, separation, and guilt learn to lie, to live in a world of "make-believe," to protect ourselves from emotional and psychological shock.

As children of domestic violence, we experience extreme feelings of separation and loss, and have a difficult time coping with these feelings in a healthy fashion. We are terrified of being abused ourselves or becoming the abuser; therefore, we try to be extra good because we feel responsible for the violence.

As adults, we may experience flashbacks, emotional detachment, avoidance of all reminders, fear recurrence, abusive marriages, have anxiety disorders, post-traumatic disorder, and other mental-health issues.

Children of domestic violence often fail to experience the necessary developmental growth to look at alternatives to hostility; instead they withdraw and find it difficult to experience positive communication.

As a child of familial violence, I learned some lessons along the way:

1. Those who love you will violate you; therefore, as adults, we attract ourselves to others who abuse us or allow us to abuse them.

2. We are not allowed to have boundaries.

3. We are conditioned to believe we do not have personal power.

4. Violence is permissible when other avenues do not work.
5. It's not safe to trust ourselves.
6. Carrying into adulthood a child's make-believe magical world can bring about addictions, and/or a mental illness or two.

Children enact their parents' feelings and emotions. A fundamental difference between feelings and emotions is that feelings are experienced consciously, while emotions manifest either consciously or subconsciously.

The external environment a child is experiencing in the womb, and at birth through age five, is extremely influential in the child's belief systems and attitudes about the world around them and themselves.

Our brain is 90% developed by the time we are five years old. Brain development is impacted by the quality of experiences in the first few years of our life, and our children's lives.

It takes dedication, strength, determination, gratitude, and faith in yourself and God to let go of this conditioning, to stop intellectualizing with your ego mind and feel the emotions of grief, sadness, fear, anger, guilt, and rage.

Albert Einstein said, "Everything is energy and that's all there is to it. Match the frequency of the reality you want, and you cannot help but get that reality. It can be no other way. This is not philosophy, this is physics."

"Everything depends on your attitude toward yourself. That which you will not affirm as true of yourself can never be realized by you, for attitude alone is the necessary condition by which you realize your goal."

This is the reason it is so important to keep your notebook handy and write out questions and search yourself for the answers. Knowledge is power.

Begin with these questions to ask yourself. After a little practice with this technique, you will have inquiries on your own. This is how you discover what beliefs you live through your life experiences, now, and what beliefs you need to change to be healthy.

1. What do I believe about myself?
2. Do I truly believe that all I can attract myself to is abusive situations? (This cannot be so if you are asking yourself these questions).
3. I have boundaries; what are they?
4. What does personal power mean to me?
5. Is violence the only way for me to solve life's problems? What does my heart say I could otherwise do?
6. I have survived domestic violence and child abuse; no matter how I did it, can I trust myself to land on my feet now? (Yes, you can!)
7. What magical thinking and/or fairytales do I believe today, that helped me survive the brutality, but that now hold me back from experiencing life as an empowered adult?
8. What would happen if I surrendered in gratitude to the feelings and emotions of my childhood experiences that haunt me today?

I continued to live in magical thinking well into my adulthood. I grieved for years, remembering those moments on the sidewalk of my childhood home. I wasn't strong enough and I was not as magical as I believed I was. I couldn't save my family! Being an adult, magical thinking got me exactly what I felt about myself — repeated loss of relationships and grief.

If any of you lacks wisdom, let him ask of God, who gives generously to all without reproach, and it will be given to him.
—James 1:5

Begin to do random acts of kindness for yourself: maybe a professional massage? It's called massage *therapy* for a reason. A Reiki treatment or two tremendously helps in this healing process!

25
NARCISSISTIC PARENTS

CHILDREN OF NARCISSISTIC parents have their sense of self eroded and annihilated in childhood. A narcissistic parent usually displays a grandiose self-image and a good reputation, but in the four corners of their world, they are cold and indifferent to their children and spouse. They teach their children to accept interpersonal danger as the norm. Therefore, children of narcissistic parents are drawn into dangerous situations with folks who are rarely consistent in character or integrity. These children feel oddly familiar in an unsafe comfort zone in adulthood.

One morning, when I was about eight years old, I stood beside the bed in my bedroom, and noticed a gnawing feeling in my stomach, I pulled up my shirt to look at my belly. I didn't see anything causing such a twisted feeling. I pulled my shirt down, resigning myself to the belief that this is how it feels to be alive.

Delores, my natural mother was physically abusive to her children and expected them to protect her from the wrath of her husband, my father., who had homicidal tendencies, especially if he had been drinking. Yet, Dad never laid a hand on us kids.

My adopted mother, though, was the narcissistic in that family and she had seven-and-a-half years before I came on the scene to make my adopted sister Barb into a narcissist. I didn't realize I had been with two narcissistic personalities until much later in life. When this awareness came, I understood why Mrs. Mc severely punished me and allowed Barb to beat me, cut me with knifes, stab me with pencils and leave deep, bleeding scratches on my face.

My job there was to supply both of them with what their emotional need demanded on any given day. As a child, I didn't understand why "mom" didn't punish my sister for hurting me like that. Now, I understand she enjoyed watching it.

Consequently, as a child and an adult, I walked through deep depressions, self-hatred, and not feeling "good enough."

If you want to know if one or both of your parents were of the narcissistic personality, go to YouTube and search for narcissistic personality traits. Or you can go to Amazon and look for books that will help you unravel some of the mysteries of this type of environment, if that's what you experienced as a child.

In a relationship with this type of personality, there really is no room for you. I can say from experience that the dominant feeling or emotion that narcissists exhibit is indifference. They usually are quite charming socially and appear successful in the world. Behind closed doors, they are a terror to live with.

After a while with my new mother, I felt like I was a doll that sat alone on a shelf, with a faint smile on my face, demanding nothing from no one, to be taken down and displayed as a possession in public. But when the curtains went down, back on the shelf I'd go, and I better not utter a word about being uncomfortable or voicing a need I may have. I was to be extremely grateful for anything she gave me, and that included the bare necessities of clothing, attention, and indifference. Kindness occasionally, when certain associates and friends were looking.

In early adulthood I saw myself as a mechanical being wrapped in flesh. If the skin on my body was cut and bleeding, that was only so that no one would know that inside, I was nothing more than oiled apparatuses and moving gears. That image of myself disappeared when I left religious traditions behind and began a personal spiritual journey.

Moving through your armor of shields and the protection you put in place as a child is a pathway to attain knowledge and provides you with choices to decide which belief systems you want to keep and which ones you feel no longer serve your life today.

It is extremely important for you to become willing to assimilate into your consciousness and feeling self that there is a Universal and Spiritual power alive inside you, that can endow you with intelligent insights beyond the knowledge attained in the experiences of childhood abuse. It's here, for the asking, to help you, me, and all humans on this earth. Whatever manifestation or appearance your Higher Power arrives in, you will know it, for when you are in Its presence, you will "feel" lighter.

Maybe begin with nature to discover your Higher Power. Even in the city, one can go for a walk in the sun or moon light, breathing the air, feeling your body move, witnessing a bird or squirrel being what it is. Allow your eyes to drink in the colors you see. Tune into the sounds twirling around you. Squarely look at the people passing by or waiting for a bus or cab; notice their facial expressions, the gaze in their eyes. Just walk for a while. Allow yourself to feel!

Another great tool for relaxation and allowing yourself to become acquainted with a Power greater than yourself is a breathing meditation, like this one:

Sit quietly and in a comfortable chair for as long as you can. Slowly, inhale to the count of seven, hold for the count of seven, exhale to the count of seven. Just focus on how your breath feels when you inhale and how it feels when you exhale. This can be quite relaxing.

Going past your old limits is like doing stretching exercises; do a little at a time until you can work yourself into a full stretch.

As an adult, I have discovered that believing there is a God, Higher Power, or Source was not so easy at first, for the environment I experienced as a child taught me to feel God is not here. Most the folks I have mentored, in the beginning of our work together, found it difficult to acknowledge there is a loving God within them.

In a deep part of yourself, you may believe you are responsible for what happened to you. You were conditioned to believe that. But it's not your fault! You may deny what happened. You may believe you could have done something back there to stop it. A child does not have the power to do so!

Your army of self-deceptions, shields, and protections may begin deploying. You have created this army to protect your boundaries. Do you believe you can trust yourself? You must command your army! Since you created this force, you can move it, you can change it, you can make friends with it! You can send it away! Ask for willingness! Ask for insight! Ask for bravery! Ask for guidance! Then say, "Thank you."

Moving past your childlike beliefs requires effort, discomfort, faith, bravery, the act of willingness and courage, pen and paper. Begin to realize that your painful feelings are your sole responsibility to heal. No one else can heal your emotional wounds but you, even those that were too painful to deal with when you were a child. You have lived in discomfort, courage, and faith, remember that's how you lived through it as a kid? Now, you're doing it as an adult with power. Now, you have knowledge. Now, and this is the exciting part, you get to make choices about what you believe about yourself!

Writing down these questions, asking for guidance, feeling them, being authentic, may help you begin to transcend your parental idealization.

Do I believe I am responsible for what happened to me?
What beliefs did my caretakers teach me about myself?
Do I believe everything they taught me about myself?
What do I believe about myself?

After working through these questions (it may take you a couple of days), ask yourself the first question again: Do I believe I am responsible for what happened to me?

> **"Feelings trigger thoughts. Some thoughts drive actions. Being ignorant of what feelings are driving your thoughts and actions is being emotionally unaware."**
> —Krishna Saagar Rao

26
WHAT'S YOUR NAME?

Hello, Let me introduce myself.

My name is Addiction.

Some things you need to understand as we journey together:

You need me.

How will you recognize me? Only in complete despair.

My eyes will look somewhat like yours, darkened, red with rippling bags and encumbered with a hard coldness.

Eventually, you'll be able to see the deceit and hatred I feed from.

Shhh, I'm a secret to be kept in the confines of your body, mind, and spirit.

I'll protect you, for I am patient, cunning, baffling, and powerful.

K. D. Cannon

I won't desert you.

I'll involve work, play, friends, spouse, family, your children, too!

For the more allies you have the more strength I have.

You can call on me anytime, as I'm your friend.

Be assured, I'll gladly respond, empowering you with pain, confusion, fear, loneliness, degradation, hopelessness, rage, and hatred.

I need you.

Yes, we are going to be the best of friends.

Oh, by the way, my name is Addiction.

27
THE MAKING OF A CODEPENDENT

AT AGE FOUR, I witnessed my less than one-year-old brother struggling in his crib with a clear plastic bag over his entire body when I walked into his bedroom. I remember the fireman coming to save him. I know today, because I saved my baby brother's life, the outcome for my mother would have been much different.

Naturally a child feels they are the center of the world in which they live. I lived in a realm where it was my responsibility to feed my sisters and brother, change diapers, and keep all of us outside in good weather so dad wouldn't beat mom if the house was messy when he got home from work. When dad was taken away by the police for throwing knifes into the floor and waving a gun around, he told me to take care of the family while he was gone. I was less than five years old.

My role in the adopted family was being the scapegoat for all their struggles and do my best to please all four of them, and at the same time, somehow survive the attitude of indifference from all family members, including aunts, uncles, and grandparents. I was expected to be "perfect," because for the least infraction in misbehaving I was physically, emotionally, and spiritually abused. Therefore, I learned to do my best to please others and make sure everyone was comfortable. Tall orders for a seven-and-a-half-year-old child just coming out of three-and-a-half years in an orphanage. But, hey, they believed they were doing their Christian duty, right?

On the upside of these experiences, making sure everyone was comfortable at my own expense turned out to be a gift as an adult in my beauty industry career. I could easily adjust myself to the emotional climate of my clients, which made them feel very comfortable and afforded me a very good living!

Today, working in retail, I am in contact with almost all the customers who come through the doors of Walmart. They feel comfortable to share their stories with me because once again I utilize my well-honed survival techniques into a means of making a living for myself. Believe me, I am damn good at it!

What survival techniques have you acquired in your childhood environment that serve you well today?

Codependency affects your ability to have healthy, mutually satisfying relationships. This emotional and behavioral conditioning affects all your close and intimate relationships. It's an addiction, for it is formed in one-sided, emotionally destructive, and/or physically abusive conditions, which usually begins in childhood.

I was taught from birth that relationships are one-sided. Within an intimate relationship, I was the one doing most of the work to maintain it. When I would stop doing the labor it takes to sustain the connection, it would fall apart. I discovered that it takes two to build a respectful, loving, and comforting relationship. Jeez, what an awakening that was!

I felt a deep unwarranted responsibility and loyalty to others, no matter how I was treated by them. I always tried to walk a mile in the other person's shoes, which isn't a bad thing, but being overly understanding and compassionate toward another person to the extent of allowing myself to be mistreated is, well, not respecting myself!

I didn't take any responsibility for the positive outcomes that took place in my life. I would say things like, "It was so-and-so who made that possible for me." Changing that wasn't easy at first, as I felt I was betraying "others," whoever they may be, if I took any credit for what I had accomplished on my own.

Ask yourself these questions: Have I had opportunities presented to me that I made a choice to utilize and brought me success? Did I give someone else the credit for the work I did to achieve my objective? How have I discounted myself?

News Flash! You are the one who made the decision to act on what was being provided for you! Stop giving the credit you deserve to others

You are not responsible for the decisions and actions of others, only yours. This may be new information for you.

When I entered a twelve-step program for codependency, I saw myself putting folks in a spoon, holding the spoon over the hot flame of a candle, melting individuals down and injecting them into my veins. I understand this metaphor sounds shocking, because addiction to people is real!

I had to first recognize that I walked in a darkness that entailed great fear. I couldn't deny it anymore. I was hardly functioning; even doing simple, everyday tasks were becoming very difficult. When I began to tell my "secrets," to the twelve-step group, I was able to begin to "feel" the emotions I had suppressed for so long. I had to become willing not to hide anything and to enter communion with my feelings. It was frightening, because I believed my feelings would destroy me if I allowed them to surface.

I learned how to set boundaries that were loving to others and protected me. When there was a family gathering, I would accept the invitation, then within myself I would set a time limit of how long I would be with them and made sure that I had something else planned that day so that I could truthfully say to them when it was time to go that I had to be somewhere else.

I experienced all kind of waking nightmares, shedding the secrets of my childhood life. I would see men coming through the walls of my apartment, dressed in trench coats and wearing brimmed hats. Their eyes were beady and black, and their teeth were shaped like those of a shark. They carried knives and chains and they were going to kill me. My unwarranted loyalties were supported by the emotions of guilt and shame for letting the skeletons out of the closet.

My ego created these tricks that appeared so real, to protect my conscious mind. That's what the ego is designed for, and its deception is to draw us into intellectualizing our feelings instead of "feeling our feelings" using fear (false evidence appearing real), to draw us away from our truth. Magical thinking does not always come wrapped in a beautiful fairy tale, especially when one is working through the "feelings" of a living nightmare.

Through the process of telling my tale, feeling my feelings, eventually the monsters disappeared into nothingness!

In codependent relationships, the more dominant personality uses emotional blackmail to control the other and appears detached and/or indifferent to their partner, friends, children, or co-workers. It "looks" as if they have all the power.

They usually always have an excuse as to why they are doing what is uncomfortable or down-right painful to others in their world, and that excuse is, "… if it wasn't for that person, situation or institution, I wouldn't have done that or be this way…." Blah, blah, and more blah.

Don't let this fool you! Whether you are the passive or dominant actor of an unhealthy codependent life, it all boils down to a relationship built on a foundation of fear, guilt, and shame — on both sides. Usually, in codependent relationships, one "appears" to be the grasshopper and one "appears" to be the giant. These roles can be exchanged between partners.

Dealing with this is not comfortable work. You will walk through tremendous pain and fear. It is the only way, but there will be a great release into the joy of inner peace and strength that you didn't know resided within you!

I mentored a young woman who intellectualized her feelings. This was her ego talking, around in circles, through the bushes, and back down into the rabbit hole: repeating the same stories of drama taking place in her life, talking very fast and every other word was utter profanities. When we use language like this, it's because we don't know the language of feelings or we are so angry we can't think of words to use to describe to ourselves and someone else what we are feeling. Her intellectual binges were huge signs of her fear to feel her feelings. Her ego told her "feeling" what happened to her would destroy her life. When she broke through all the mind chatter and began to feel, she would physically become uncomfortable and sometimes ill. This was her ego's way of "protecting" her psyche from what happened to her in childhood. We all go through this phase in the healing process.

In one of our sessions together, she told me she had entered the "dark night of her soul." She told me she had walked through her feelings, felt them, and had now accepted that what happened in her childhood, really happened to her. Breakthrough!

Within a few weeks she began implementing the tools she learned along the way to take care of herself with those who abused her for thirty-seven years. Her intention was to free herself of the enmeshments of codependency and still maintain her familial relationships.

Within a couple months of this awakening and taking the most loving and peaceful path she could with her family, she began to set boundaries by saying "NO" to what they wanted her to do for them and "YES" to what she wanted for her and her own children's lives! Now, she is no longer blown by the wind of the wishes and whims of others.

Bonus here, folks! She now detaches herself from the behaviors of her friends and family in order to allow them to learn from the natural consequences of their actions!

She has identified and immobilized generational abuse in its tracks!

> **"For there is nothing hidden that will not be disclosed, and nothing concealed that will not be known or brought out into the open."**
>
> —Luke 8:17

28
PETS?

I REMEMBER THERE was a small dog in my family of origin. The only thing I remember about that dog is that we were all sitting at the dinner table; the dog wanted outside, and my dad let him out.

The family that adopted me had a dog, Pesty. She was medium-sized, lots of fur and black and white. She was frisky. I don't remember playing with her. She was chained to an insulated and heated doghouse under a tree right next to the back door. I don't remember anyone playing with her.

Dad Mc custom-built her doghouse because we lived on a lake and in the wintertime, it got really cold out there. He seemed to be the only one in the house who cared about Pesty.

Sometimes when I think of her, I feel sad because I wasn't allowed to love her. If I paid attention to her, I would be punished.

There is a photograph of me with a cat when I was about eight years old. I don't remember having any pets of my own as a child. Barb had the pets. She didn't take care of them. She ignored them most the time.

As an adult, I have had six cats and three dogs. All of them I loved very much and treated very well. I have three rescue cats today and they are quite spoiled. I've found that I lean toward rescuing animals. They depend on us as their owners to feed them, supply them with a warm place to live and, yes, believe it or not, provide emotional support.

I find great comfort being near animals. They love unconditionally. I have found that pets can bring soothing comfort to us.

Elf, he's with me now, was no longer wanted by his previous owner. To get him in the cat carrier to bring him home, we had to trick him with his favorite treats. He cried in the car on the way back to my house. I cried with him because I understood how he felt about being taken away from a home he loved.

When I got home with him, he hid under my bed and cried for four days straight for Cecilia, his previous owner. When he finally let me hold him, I promised him he would never have to go through this again, he would be with me for the rest of his life. Elf and I are very close.

In my farming days, Ben, an extremely abused Australian shepherd, was brought to me. This guy was one mean son-of-a-bitch! Fur was missing from the underside of his body, he was filthy, hungry, and afraid. I had to chain him inside the garage next to the house where I could keep an eye on him. I would go out to feed him and he would lunge at me, snarling and baring his big white teeth! I would say to him in a low, calm voice, "You shouldn't try to bite the hand that feeds you."

After a few weeks of this, I took him to the back barn, where we were holding two-month-old pigs, making sure they were healthy before we put them with the herd of their age and size. That's where Ben and I began building trust in one another. I would go out twice a day with broth with meat in it, he wasn't on a chain any longer, he was in a corral. I stayed with him for at least thirty minutes each visit just talking to him in a manner that one chats with a friend. After about four to six weeks I took him for a walk around the farm with me, and he never left my side from that day on. He trusted me so much that he would allow me to pick him up and put him in the pond, where once he got over his fear of it, he enjoyed swimming. I loved him and he loved me. There was an understanding between us. We both knew what it was like to be left behind.

When Ben died, I felt numb.

Then there was Kit-Kat. She was a survivor. She was part Himalayan and Siamese. She lived in the basement of the farmhouse, because my husband at the time didn't want her in the house. I often forgot she was down there. When my husband and I separated I took her with me, and she blossomed into a beautiful, loving pet. She had a couple of litters and they all were dominantly Siamese. She was a trouper, for sure. She moved to another state with me and there another abandoned kitten came into our life.

Miss Margaret, a Blue Russian, was about six weeks old when she was found in an abandoned car. Boy oh boy, Kit Kat did not like her at first. While I was at work, I had to keep Kit Kat outside because I was afraid she would kill Miss Margaret if I wasn't in the house with them together. I had to feed Miss Margaret canned cat food mixed with milk, like a cereal we make for our own babies when they begin to eat solid foods.

Miss Margaret was very sensitive and seemed to understand when I spoke to her. She remained a kitten, even though fully grown, until she was about two years old. She and Kit Kat were both indoor/outdoor cats. Miss Margaret didn't have a litter of kittens until she was more than two years old. When she did, she talked to them all the time, just like I talked to her all the time when she was a kitten. She loved sleeping on my back at night. She, too, traveled with me when I moved back home to Michigan.

Kit Kat was Michigan-born and buried in Colorado. Miss Margaret was born in Colorado and buried in Michigan. These two pets were with me when I discovered I was bipolar, an alcoholic, and very emotionally ill.

They often were my personal support-system. We loved each other very much. They love me more unconditionally than I loved them, because they put up with my mood swings, which could be very uncomfortable for all of us.

Once, Miss Margaret was acting very strange, so I took her to the vet. I was told she was having a nervous breakdown. I learned from that experience, that like our children, pets also reflect our emotions.

I have a deep compassion for abused or abandoned animals. I understand how they feel and when I take one into my home, they are treated with respect and great love.

I have found that animals also have memories; that abandoned and/or abused animals do have flashbacks. Like Elf, when someone comes to visit, he hides so they cannot take him away. Boo, the youngest of the three I have now, was found in the woods, screaming. I heard him and saw that it was this little tiny kitten barely seen because of the tall weeds. I squatted down, opened my arms, and said, "Come here, little Boo." He jumped over the tall weeds, made it to my leg, from there climbed up my body to my shoulder and hung on for dear life. He's been with me for nine years now. Elf is his adopted dad. Elf taught him to hide with guests are in our home.

A friend brought Catfish to me because his owners decided they wanted dogs, too. The dogs were mauling Catfish. He has claws and has put holes in bedspreads and I'm still working with him about sharpening his claws on my Lazy Boy recliner. He would scream at me every morning, until one morning I told him in my sternest tone of voice that I was tired of that and if he didn't change it up, I was going to throw his ass out the door. He only does it occasionally now. I can live with that.

Our pets understand, they feel, they intuit, and they know things, just like we do.

29
BLACKOUTS AND ALCOHOL ADDICTION

> "Addiction was the inverse of honest work. It was everything, right now. I drank away nervousness, and I drank away boredom, and I needed to build a new tolerance. Yes, to discomfort, yes to frustration, yes to failure, because it meant I was getting stronger. I refused to be the person who only played games she could win."
> —Sarah Hepola, *Blackout: Remembering the Things I Drank to Forget*

DISSOCIATION CAN BE defined as disruptions in aspects of consciousness, identity, memory, physical actions, and/or environment.

Dissociation as avoidance-coping usually happens because of a traumatic event. Being powerless to do anything to change or stop a shocking event may lead us to disconnect from the situation to cope with feelings of helplessness, fear, or pain. Dissociation can help us get through to the end of the harrowing experience.

Did you experience blackouts as a kid, or remove your awareness from the situation through daydreaming, leaving only your body in the room, not your consciousness?

The Merck Manual defines localized amnesia, as, "… being unable to recall specific event or events or a specific period: these gaps in memory are usually related to trauma or stress. For example, patients may forget the months or years of being abused as a child or the days spent in intense combat…."

Living in the war zone of my parent's relationship, and later, in a family of emotional indifference, I became disassociated from my emotional and physical bodies. The feeling I felt for years felt like a piece of fabric twisted very tightly that rumbled just below my belly button and felt like a festering, burning sore in a vacuum of darkness and terrifying emotional shadows.

I felt deep loneliness that couldn't be filled and a separation from other people.

Is there a place in your body where you feel that something very uncomfortable is making its home there?

In bouts of childhood amnesia. operating on autopilot, the subconscious mind records all that is happening around us, whether we remember or not. I remember my first year of school with my adopted family, I was in the second grade, that's when I met Dagmar. She was my best friend in school until I dropped out at sixteen years old. The summer between second and third grade, Barb and I were outside playing, and I began to cry and couldn't stop, we went in the house for Mom to help me. I couldn't explain to her why I was crying. She suggested that I walk up to our mailbox. Our driveway was about an eighth of a mile long. We lived in the country. I made her promise that she would be there when I got back with the mail. She wasn't. No one was, not Barb, not Granny, not Mom, everyone disappeared while I was gone. I called out to them, no one answered. I began to climb the stairs to see if they were in the bedrooms upstairs. As I took one step at a time up the stairs, I saw a blanket of darkness come over my mind. I do not remember reaching the top of those stairs or anything about the rest of that summer or the third grade, or the summer between the third and fourth grades. When conscious awareness became available to me again, I was sitting in my fourth-grade classroom, sitting next to another student, Martha Hippio. I asked her what was going on. She told me that I was being voted editor of our fourth-grade newspaper because everyone in the class liked talking with me. I don't remember one damn thing about anything leading up to that moment, except the climbing of those stairs and the blanket of darkness that floated over my mind months earlier. As a child, I must have functioned quite well when the darkness came.

Hark! There is a place in your unconscious mind that remembers!

The unconscious mind never sleeps, it does not go into blackouts. It records everything that goes on around you. It is the conscious mind that is the analyzer. If it cannot make sense of what's happening around you or to you, it will protect itself through your ego using blackouts, amnesia, extenuating magical thinking, getting stuck in a fairy tale, and/or experiencing addictions that "appear" to bring relief from the realities of your childhood and current experiences that your mind may have suppressed. This survival mode is the true function of your ego, to keep you alive!

When I took my first drink of alcohol, I was sixteen years old, I liked it so much, I became drunk and went into a blackout. I felt no cause for alarm, as I was used to blackouts in childhood. For me they were a natural occurrence of being alive. Anesthetizing myself through alcohol blackouts, I had created an escape from unbearable emotional discomfort. I believed, as an adult, the use of alcohol for self-induced shutdowns were my friends. How many times did blackouts save my sanity as a child?

Today, I wonder how did I survive the insanity of this belief system as an adult?

- Do you drink until you black out, finding the blackouts to feel familiar? Possibly a relief?
- Do you believe that everyone blacks out when they drink?
- Do you feel that blackouts are a normal part of life?
- The day after blackout drinking, do you sense you did something wrong in the blackout?

Drinking alcohol and using drugs are great indicators of living in fear.

After two years of being in a twelve-step program for codependence, the adult child, parent, spouse or friend of an alcoholic, I became aware that I am also an alcoholic. I only drank every few years, but when I did, I would destroy the life I had built for myself in those sober times.

Through entering the twelve-step program of Alcoholics Anonymous, I discovered that it didn't matter how much or how little I drank alcohol, I was a manic-depressive (bi-polar) blackout drinker, who relived over and over the destruction of my family through demolishing my life every few years! Amazing! I lived the past repeatedly and somehow managed not to commit suicide!

Is there some piece of your past that you feel you just can't escape, that keeps showing up in your life today?

When I entered AA, my relationship with God was still intact, steeped in fear. I was raised in a faith pronouncing that God was angry and vengeful with his most wonderful creation, humans. There was no way any living person could make that better because all of us are born sinners, will die sinners, and Jesus Christ is the only person who walked this earth who was perfect in God's eyes. I felt like everyone in that church was pissed off all the time. With this kind of faith, who wouldn't be?

I learned through doing the twelve-step work that I could create a relationship with a God of my choosing.

How could I begin to change my perception of an angry and vengeful God into a peaceful, loving, Higher Power?

I used nature. I took long walks in wooded areas and sat down under trees and simply stared at their foliage. I saw each leaf as a separate world of the universe of the tree and wondered what life forms lived on each one.

I consciously inhaled the aroma of the foliage in which I sat. It smelled fresh, and alive!

I was able to feel the warm sun on my skin glowing from an azure blue sky decorated with fluffy white marshmallow clouds. I began to hear nature buzzing all around me.

I hugged a tree, feeling the rough, cool bark on my face and bare arms. I imagined its sap flowing up through my body, cleansing me of tension and negativity. I felt myself connected to its throbbing roots deep in the earth. My arms, hands, and fingers became its branches stretching high into the sky, touching the face of a loving and caring Source!

I felt I was being infused with love and life! I still hug trees today. They have so much love to share!

I suggest that you hug a tree. I know, I know, it sounds a little strange, but tree hugging has been shown to soothe and strengthen the body and mind. Simply seeing trees makes us feel calmer, leading to lower heart rate and blood pressure. Plus, hugging a tree (just like hugging a human), increases levels of oxytocin, aka the love hormone, which reduces stress and increases happiness.

That's the God I choose to believe in!

One of many influential life lessons I learned from working with the twelve-steps in Ala-Non and Alcoholics Anonymous is that I have the power to make choices that serve my life in a respectful and loving manner, but I must first find a God I can believe in. We cannot have healthy relationships with folks we are afraid of; therefore, it stands to reason we cannot have a loving relationship with a God who terrorizes us.

> **"A tree says: My strength is trust. I know nothing about my fathers, I know nothing about the thousand children that every year spring out of me. I live out the secret of my seed to the very end, and I care for nothing else. I trust that God is in me. I trust that my labor is holy. Out of this trust I live."**
>
> —Herman Hesse

30
HEALING IS ON ITS WAY!

> I am an immortal being conceiving myself as man and forming worlds in the likeness and image of my concept of self.
>
> —Neville Goddard, author of
> *Awakened Imagination & the Search*

THE HEALING BEGAN for me when I was diagnosed with bipolar disorder. This is a chemical imbalance of the brain.

It was a particularly dreadful winter day. I had a horrible cold, and I couldn't stop crying or screaming. This was not normal behavior for me!

I had to force a family member to take me to the emergency room. I needed help! Something was seriously wrong!

In the doctor's report, he stated I was incapable of being responsible for myself, that I was a lost cause.

That pissed me off! I felt his judgment was harsh!

Duh, I got myself to the hospital. My actions showed that I was capable of being responsible for myself by asking for help.

Do not allow anyone to convince you that you are not capable of being worthy or that you will always, and forever be the person you are in this moment. That is never true!

I discovered this concept from Neville Goddard, "I am an immortal being conceiving myself as man and forming worlds in the likeness and image of my concept of self." In other words, it's up to you. Who do you want to be? Do you want to continue making excuses why you can't access your dreams and desires? Or, do you want to let the truth sink in: you create your world in the likeness of your thoughts, feelings, attitudes, and beliefs that you hold in your consciousness. Everything that is created, everything, begins in consciousness. Most of your beliefs are stored in your unconscious mind. Don't fret, you can access these hidden beliefs by looking at what shows up in your life today. Just sayin'.

The deepest feelings, attitudes, and beliefs systems about yourself are through the filter of indifference. As you walk back through your life, can you remember learning the feeling of indifference? Write it down.

Scientific research contends that the fetus in its mother's womb is being conditioned, through the mind, consciousness, emotions, feelings, and environment in which it was conceived; therefore, the unborn child learns how to express its attitudes, beliefs, and feelings to navigate life when it is born.

The energy in which I was spawned and birthed was "violence."

The psychiatrist who worked with me in the hospital provided tests; the results were quite illuminating and that was my first introduction to the wisdom that knowledge is power. I was inspired to alter these findings:

1. I had no roots. I was thirty-one years old, and I had no roots!

2. I responded to life as a child who had been in a war.
3. The chemical imbalance manifested itself through the emotion of violence. Dr. Rhyee explained that if I didn't do something about this, I was going to die a violent death!

I didn't like this picture so well ... I knew he was tellin' me the truth!

As he was explaining this to me, I quickly took an inventory of my life and realized there had been lots of violence.

When I began to study myself and how bipolar disorder affected my life, there were two questions to which I wanted an answer:

Is bipolar disorder, the chemical imbalance, causing the deep anger I experience?

Or does the anger, the rage, I feel cause the bipolar disorder?

For God hath not given us the spirit of fear; but of power, and of love, and of a sound mind.
—2 Timothy 1:7

As time passed, I learned that through our consciousness, energy is created in our bodies that can cause disease. (Dis-Ease). Chemical imbalance, bipolar disorder, was the physical manifestation in my physical body of the deep-rooted feelings, (energy), and images of violence in my chakra system and sub-conscious mind. They were all beliefs and attitudes I established about life in general and about myself by the age of five years old.

Science has shown that a fetus' brain is affected by the world outside the womb.

Possibly, you've reached a place of struggle, where holding on to the past is competing with letting it go.

Haven't you had moments in your life where you had courage to do things you never believed you would? It could be anything: marriage, having children, working a job that you enjoy, leaving a job you don't enjoy, white-water rafting, or maybe skydiving, or changing your belief systems to support yourself.

Your story has been your identity! It's who you believe yourself to be.

You can re-create yourself through changing your story, by changing your attitudes and beliefs about yourself. We are created to become creators!

Living your life unconsciously through the past is not only re-creating the past in your life *NOW*, but also keeps you fettered in darkness. How can we create something new for ourselves when we keep reacting to our life today from the attitudes and beliefs we incurred in the past?

Write down these questions. Read the words very slowly, allow the feelings to come to surface.

"What will I do without this story?" For a few moments imagine you don't have a story enveloping you. Look past the glittering frame, deep into the tapestry of your picture.

You won't recognize yourself at first.

Currently, you are only taking in data. Possibly, gloomy clouds of self- judgments will have moved elsewhere for a while.

"What will become of me, the me I know now, if I step across the threshold into the unknown?"

"Who am I without this story, my identity?"

Didn't you ask for this shedding of skin, to be fresh wine put into a new wine bag? You must have, you're here, Now!

"How has the pain, the suffering, the aloneness help shape you into the miraculous individual you are today?"

There are strengths you've attained, character that has been established, unique gifts provided you, and dimensions within you formed through the experience of your story. There is beauty in you today that developed through the negative experience of childhood traumas. (There's usually more than one).

Pretend you are your child self, in your favorite childhood experience, and begin daydreaming.

Then write.

There are so many talents you have gained through the processes of protecting yourself in abusive childhood experiences and conditionings. Maybe you're an empath, being capable of feeling other's emotions. More than likely you are naturally intuitive, because you had to learn to know when to duck when the shit started flying around the room in your childhood family environment.

You can choose to turn the sense of separation, deep loneliness, and fear of being alone felt in captivity of an abusive family into a sanctuary of precious healing solitude for yourself.

Hold yourself like a newborn baby child.

"No problem can be solved from the same level of consciousness that created it."

—Albert Einstein

31
AN EPIPHANY

> When I was a child, I used to speak like a child, think like a child, reason like a child; but when I grew up, I did away with childish things.
>
> —I Corinthians 13

WHEN YOU BEGIN to change your beliefs and attitudes about yourself, you may experience what I refer to as, "the battle of the soldiers." One battalion is defending the ego identity of yourself formed in childhood, but your heart has been opened, instilling new and loving self-concepts formed in spiritual truths that you desire to have inaugurated into your consciousness to support your life today.

You may expect a beautifully wrapped package with a gigantic gorgeous bow on top, being gently placed in your hands because you have made yourself willing to learn a new way of feeling about yourself and your life and you have acted on your willingness. This is not an unusual feeling about personal healing and growth, but most of the time it doesn't happen this way.

What may come instead is a sense of walking through the dark forest, not being able to see where to place one foot in front of the other, but somehow trusting you're going to receive the promise of release from inner adversaries and the childlike defenses developed long ago that no longer provide protection.

When feelings come up, especially those that are repetitive, they have something important to say, and maybe you haven't been willing to listen to them. You may want to talk with them as if they are a person standing in front of you wanting your attention. You could ask, "I'm listening. What is it you want to say to me?"

Sometimes the response can be in full sentences and sometimes there are only a few key words thrown out from the depths of your emotional being. And sometimes the feeling only wants to be acknowledged, and it floats away.

Then there may be feelings like guilt and shame that arise for no reason at all; you haven't done anything to justify these feelings. If you're not sure who or what your feelings of guilt and shame belong to, then ask: "Is this my feelings of guilt and shame, or did someone teach me to believe this about myself?" Being in an abusive situation is like being a hostage. You come to believe what your captors tell you to believe because it's how you survived it.

When you are letting go of old beliefs, you may feel like something is dying. It is. The "old" paradigm you once held dear, is your "identity," the ego mind created in childhood, usually made up of childish "defenses" that are being released to allow you to step into a world of personal, adult empowerment. It's important to listen to soothing music, watch a comedy, (to invoke laughter, because laughter heals), read a book that is uplifting for you and to meditate. When you are in your meditation, talk with those beliefs you desire to let go of. You can say something like, "Thank you for all you've done for me. I understand that you feel sad, I do too. You've been with me for as long as I can remember, and you have protected me very well. It's time for both of us to move on, so I'm sending you into the light. I love you. Good-bye."

You may have to do this a few times with some of your beliefs. Be ready, for you will be met with resistance, from your outer world, and your inner world. Be grateful for this resistance because it means you are becoming more of the person you desire to be.

Creator of *Self Mastery-The Journey Home To Your Inner Self,* Joseph Hu Dalconzo explains the "Inner Child" this way: **"It is your childlike memories and programs that are emotionally anchored to a time when you only had the power, knowledge, and physical strength of a small child. Your inner child needs to learn to trust the "adult you" because you have adult powers now that he or she didn't have. You need to make your inner child feel safe and secure."**

Often the fears, anxieties, phobias, mental illness, and addictions that surface in adulthood are providing information about your interpretations of the impressions left on you from living in adverse circumstances as a child. You had to think on your feet; feeling was not safe. You developed survival techniques that were available to you, with the one power you possessed, your imagination.

To begin to help yourself feel safe and secure in the world, please refer to the "Feel to Release" Chart for emotional distinction on page 39. First look to the column on the right to help you distinguish your emotional block, then move across the page, engaging in each feeling the best you can and write in your journal what are each of these four feelings messaging to you. This chart will help you to put the proper language in place for your emotions, opening doors for you to know yourself.

You may have lived in an assortment of environments as a child. One survival technique you may have created is a honeycomb in your mind, called compartmentalization. It eases the mental discomforts and anxieties of conflicting values, emotions, and beliefs within yourself. It allows you to hold two or more conflicting ideas that co-exist by inhibiting them to connect and interact between the separate compartmentalized self-states. The birth of the compartments may have saved your sanity and your life.

Unknowingly, I made life decisions from a child's point of view until I had this awakening:

A work associate recorded one of our phone conversations, in which I was ranting about how much I disliked our employer. The next morning this associate played it for the boss, and I was escorted out the door when I arrived at work! This is where my negative thinking and feelings took me! ICK!

Because I drove my income and living space away, I stayed at a dear friend's home for a couple of months and she prepared a meditation area for me in her basement.

One morning I entered the damp basement, the washer was swishing clothes clean and the dryer was humming and thumping them dry. I stepped over the oozing stream of water heading for the sump pump, to sit at my meditation table. Over it hung a bare, glaring light bulb.

I paused for a moment from my reading and writing, looking up into the raftered ceiling. Stark light filled my consciousness! Scales dropped from my eyes, heart, and mind. Doors opened, and for the first time I could see I was totally responsible for all the things that had taken place in my adult life. The good, the bad, and the ugly. I couldn't take my eyes off the glaring light bulb. Its illumination filled the dark caves of my soul, and I knew I was not seeing dimly into the mirror, I was looking straight into the depths of my heart. It was an epiphany!

I had summoned psycho/spiritual transformation! I became willing to do whatever was asked of me to walk out of the hell in which I lived. What I discovered about being willing, is that God was not asking me to be perfect in my willingness; I was only being asked to open my heart to willingness.

I saw I had built lives for myself, and then compulsively, torn them apart, to be left homeless and feeling all the loss I felt as a child. It was an addiction! As an adult, I had not stayed in one place for any more than three years at this point. I blamed others when my life fell apart: the job, the companion, the church, the weather, whatever or whomever was available on which to pin the responsibility of my devastation. Until my heart was opened, I was not taking responsibility for my life. I began to connect the dots that were in separate compartments and were not allowed to communicate, be interchangeable, or integrated with one another. Now, they were beginning to communicate with each other. I felt it!

The childhood conflicts between alternating values and beliefs began to diminish, for I had instilled enough loving, spiritual laws, beliefs and attitudes in my psyche that allowed me to feel safe enough to face myself. There I sat among this rearrangement of my inner foundation, and no one knew what was taking place in that closet of prayer, except Jesus and me. It was a miracle!

I unhooked my eyes from that light bulb and looked down at the table filled with books, pens, and paper. I laughed with utter joy, for I felt I had been released from a prison of blinding obsession and given power and discernment to make loving choices that would lead me back to my highest Self. I prayed, "Thank you Jehovah God, through Jesus and the Holy Spirit for this time in my life, because from my vantage point, sitting in this basement, there is nowhere to go from here but up!"

This awakening didn't happen overnight. It took a few months after being fired from my job. I did a lot of seeking and knocking on the door, tears flowed, read books, I began with Louise Hays' book, *You Can Heal Your Life,* and Ernest Holmes' book, *Love and Law.* I listened closely to my intuition, and it led me to the right books for me at the right times.

When you desire and dedicate yourself to heal your life, no matter what the obstacles, Source will give you the stamina to endure the dark nights of the soul you will experience.

Believing in miracles is solidified.

There is a peace that comes that is beyond understanding.

32

THE BUILDING OF A NEW FOUNDATION

> "For other foundation can no man lay than that is laid, which is Jesus Christ."
>
> —1 Corinthians 3:11

MY LIFE DIDN'T suddenly become hunky-dory because of the basement experience. New challenges came forth in my life. I had to learn how to implement my spiritual awakening in my day-to-day living.

I studied books written by luminaries from the post-Civil War era to the present time. I needed their wisdom and strength to navigate into and through the change of surroundings and people I would be working with and the positive experiences I wanted in life.

Just before I headed south into my new life, I went into the store on my way out of town and asked the clerk there for something that was a Christ-based teaching because I was moving to a new town, with new people, new everything and needed something to keep me focused during the adjustment period. She introduced me to Marianne Williamson. I didn't know who she was or what she taught. I followed my intuition, purchasing the CD, *Handling Fear*. Lo and behold, when I arrived in my new town, Royal Oak, Marianne was speaking on Sundays in the theater there! I met her, had a book autographed by her and discovered her teachings are based on the text, *A Course in Miracles*.

A Course in Miracles, (ACIM), published in 1976, walks its students through the meanderings of the human ego-mind. It teaches you how to let go of your rationalizations, (lies), about who you are. It includes lessons for three hundred and sixty-five days to help you break through the walls you have established that keep you separated from yourself, your fellow humans, and God. As well as reading ACIM on your own time, I would advise that if you're interested in an in-depth study of this material to attend A Course in Miracles meetings. You will have tons of a-ha moments ingesting this book!

"Attitudinal Healing" is an organization established in 1975 by Gerald G. Jampolsky, M.D., to help children with life-threatening illnesses. He wrote a best seller; *Love is Letting Go of Fear.*

Jerry states, "At any moment we can choose peace over conflict, love over fear."

I found that even though I lived alone in a beautiful apartment, in a fabulous city, with a wonderful income, I constantly heard the adults of my childhood screaming. When I arrived at Attitudinal Healing meetings, I was still holding on to lots of anger. For the first year and a half this loving and patient group guided me into letting go of the fears, which ended the screaming in my mind. Again, I was given more inner peace.

There are layers of pain and hurt you endured as a child, then compounded in adulthood, not yet knowing that you had choices in what to believe about yourself. Peace comes through the heart, not your intellect. Like prescribed medicine, bringing your spirit, emotions, body, and mind into balance, peace comes in doses, to move you along into letting go more and more of your unkind ideas and feelings about yourself created in childhood and preparing yourself to receive your gifts of peace. These include dismantling fears, loss of the separated feelings, and connecting you deeper into your heart This then brings you to a meaningful understanding of the proper use of your ego-mind, gently leads you to listen to your spirit or intuition more than your ego for guidance on your journey, makes your life much easier. Peace will direct you on the road to establishing autonomy from your caretakers in childhood.

Possibly, you have had years of secular psychological training. Maybe you were as Humpty Dumpty who fell off the wall.

While in my first stable home, I began to incorporate psychological and spiritual principles through the practice of Unity principles, which supported A Course in Miracles and Attitudinal Healing teachings. For the first time in my life I was beginning to grow roots! And I lived in this home for eight years! The longest time I lived anywhere in my life!

Unity aims to demonstrate that the teachings of Jesus Christ can be lived every day. Its followers believe that the true «Church» is a state of consciousness in humankind.

> " **Unity teaches that each person is a unique expression of God, that each person is sacred, and each person is worthy.**"
>
> —Wikipedia

The subconscious mind is like the womb. It is impregnated by our conscious thoughts and feelings, then forms attitudes or assumptions that we consciously or unconsciously believe about ourselves. These often manifest in our physical lives at some point, maybe years after the seed has been planted.

The subconscious mind does not question what the conscious mind sends to it. It receives the message and begins to work on creating it for us. Consciousness is the only reality. What we see in the physical world is ever-changing because consciousness is continuously changing.

Do we breathe ourselves? Do we think about how to move the muscles in our bodies when we need to move? Do we tell our heart muscle that it needs to pump the blood through our veins for nourishment and life? Do we have to instruct our skeletal structure to support our tissues, organs, and skin? No!

The autonomic nervous system is a control system that acts largely unconsciously and regulates bodily functions. We have been wonderfully created!

The subconscious mind is an all-seeing and hearing mechanism. Even when we're asleep, it is collecting data from everything going on around us.

One reason why subliminal messages work so well is because the conscious mind can't hear them, therefore it can't argue about them or block them with its noisy chatter.

The mind is the "I AM" of who we are.

The conscious mind is only the tip of the iceberg of consciousness, the one we can easily see. The subconscious is the large mass beneath it that runs the whole show. It only creates what it is instructed to create through our thoughts and feelings. It never questions. It works from our assumptions about everything we experience in life. How we react or how we respond to our circumstances directs the subconscious mind to create our feelings and beliefs in our physical world.

> "What things so ever you desire, when you pray, believe that you receive them, and you shall have them."
> —Mark 11:24

By the way, worrying, which is unloving and negative energy, is also praying.

When you imagine your dreams, put gigantic emotions into the dreaming process. Feel and know it's yours NOW!

Example: I feel the excitement of being the first owner of the vehicle of my dreams; driving it off the lot with only a few miles on the odometer; its exterior is red, and its interior is grey or black. I luxuriate in the heated leather seats. It has four-wheel drive, automatic transmission, I'm singing at the top of my lungs to the killer stereo system, it includes a CD player, I feel the air conditioning flowing over my skin, my phone is connected to its wi-fi and the is GPS is providing driving directions. To top it off, it has an extended bumper to bumper warranty. I look in the rear-view mirror of my new SUV and see my loved ones sitting in the backseat, smiling. We're going for a ride in the new vehicle! Oh, by-the-way, this new ride is fully paid for; I am debt-free!

Writing out your desires gives your spoken words more power than you can imagine, because they are words you can see, as well as hear yourself speak.

Writing out your dreams also gives you time to truly feel the feelings you would feel if the desired thing manifested in your life. Do this at a quiet time, so there is room to explore your emotions, and change the wording if it doesn't feel exactly right to you. Writing also formulates your desires into an image that you can focus on throughout your day. This book is peppered with ideas for meditation, breathing, and writing exercises. All these methods will help you to create the glorious life you dream of living.

Do your best not to become anxious about fulfilling your desires. If you are anxious, you are not trusting your Higher Power, which is truly your Source of all that comes to you. When you follow your intuition's lead, you will experience manifestations in your physical world that are far better than what you thought could be possible. Detaching from outcomes makes your life a whole lot easier. And having a sense of humor makes living lighter. Keep your mind focused on what is your heart's desires and allow Spirit to lead you on the plain path into your new life.

33
COMING FULL CIRCLE

COMING FULL CIRCLE kind of feels like déjà vu. It's an experience we have in the present time of life that resembles an experience we had in the past. It can feel surreal. It happens to remind us to come back and ground ourselves in our Creator.

At Christmas time in the orphanage, the Big Brothers and Sisters organization would come and celebrate the holidays, playing games with us and bringing goodies to enjoy.

One Christmas I was playing with a hula-hoop, I tripped over it and hit the floor, putting my front teeth through my lower lip, which left a lifetime scar.

Six decades later this happened again in my bathtub while showering. I stepped in the shower, lost my balance, fell and once again put my front teeth through my lower lip. Now, I have two scars.

I felt three energy levels at once. I was in the present moment, attending to the new wound; I was in the past, a hurting and fearful child being taken to the hospital for stitches; and I was in the future, knowing, feeling something important just happened that would change my life forever.

Then my ego-mind took over for a bit.

I was pissed that I did this to myself-again!

I was afraid I had created something that was going to destroy my life, because I saw a flash from the past, a child, me, tripping and falling, putting my front teeth through my lower lip!

First, I gave myself reprimands spoken in the language of profanity.

Then....

I breathed, calming all energy bodies, helping me to surrender to gratitude. (I wrote, "I surrender into gratitude" on my bathroom mirror months before this happened).

Then I could listen....

Intuitively, I felt this had something to do with me learning a spiritual law and truth.

In the orphanage, when a child got hurt or there was an accident, there wasn't a loving parent there to hold us until we felt better. There was an efficient staff member who made sure the children were taken care of according to state laws.

I took myself to a nearby hospital to have the new wound taken care of. I called my daughter to let her know what happened. She was with me in the emergency room within an hour of my call and stayed with me the rest of the day until late evening.

When my daughter walked into the emergency room, the nurse smiled a huge smile and told me, "Your daughter's here." I immediately felt a deep inner shift. I was no longer a lonely little orphan girl. I was all grown up, with a caring family surrounding me. When she walked into the room, it lit up! I was reminded once again that I had taken myself and my child out of the cycle of generational abuse and with it came perks. Authentic respect and love between family members. My heart's desire had been given to me! And as a side bonus,

I could see that I needed first to learn how to nurture myself at times like this.

As you journey on your path to healing your childhood wounds, you will find yourself in situations that are mirroring past experiences. Your intuition, through coming full circle, is leading you out of those old thoughts, beliefs, and feelings about yourself by showing you the love you have manifested in your world today. And, that, my friend, is where we are the most blinded!

Now, don't get your panties in a wad when you read the next sentence. Coming full circle may lead you to an understanding that what happened to you in childhood was a blessing. Let's look at this: If you were removed from your parents' care, could there have been something much more dangerous going on than your child mind could acknowledge? Could there have been physical violence between your parents, between siblings and parents, parents inflicting physical abuse on you and your siblings? Were there chemical addictions being practiced in your childhood home? Do you recall any weapons you may have seen one or both of your parents threatening the household? Did your parents violate you with emotional distance? Were you made to feel responsible for your parents and siblings, if you had siblings? Did emotional and/or physical sexual abuse from your immediate family or other family members appear to be normal behavior?

If you were a child who was removed from your parents' custody, maybe for a short period of time, maybe for a long while or maybe forever, have you allowed yourself to discover the truth through your feelings as to why this happened? Remember, feelings never lie.

Ask yourself: What kind of person would I be today if I had been allowed to stay with my family?

You may believe you wouldn't have had so many problems throughout your adulthood had you been raised within your natural family. But in fact, you may have had a lot more problems if your parents had raised you.

I was married to a man who physically abused me. At first, I didn't recognize that I had married my father and had become my mother in this relationship. A black eye, and a few doctor visits later, I left this situation. I have not put myself in this type of environment again. Even though I wasn't going to church or studying a bible, Spirit moved me from the inside out to be able to distinguish that I wasn't living the life I was intended to live. I was living my parents' life. I had come full circle.

Now, I began walking through autonomy.

There are probably many ways you have come full circle that you may or may not be aware of -yet.

Possibly you could look at your situation through a different lens, one with a little gratitude for how far you have come. Asking "why" keeps you in victim mode. Asking how you can change how you now feel about your background is the important question. Looking over your adult life, where did you come full circle in an intimate relationship? Were you in a relationship that reflected your parents' relationship? What happened that woke you up? Were you physically abused by your partner? Did you physically abuse your partner? Were you emotionally available in your relationships? Were others you were in relationship with emotionally available to you? Were your partner or you practicing addicts? How about your children, was there something you may have done to your children that was unkind, then one day you saw and felt that this had been done to you as a child and you stopped doing it? Can you see where you might have unconsciously in your adulthood mimicked feelings, then took actions on what you were taught in childhood? Can you recall an ah-ha moment that brought you to an acute awareness that you were emotionally mistaken or blinded in your beliefs about yourself through negative childhood conditioning? Once the blinders came off, were you able to see that you are living a more supportive and loving life today? Did you feel a release into joy for witnessing what you had accomplished? You took lemons and made lemonade with them! This is coming full circle.

Maybe if you hadn't been removed from your parents' custody, you could have matured into a pedophile or serial killer or spent your life in prison or in a mental institution. Being placed in a foster or group home provided you with a warm bed to sleep in, a roof over your head and food to eat. You were a child when this happened to you, there is no way that you could have provided these necessities for yourself. This may be a place to begin to work with the feeling of gratitude. Just sayin.'

I Thessalonians 5:18 says, **"In everything give thanks: for this is the will of God in Christ Jesus concerning you."**

I understand this sounds strange considering what you have been through.

Coming full circle may lead you naturally into forgiveness in an area of your life. What I mean by natural forgiveness is that you are not aware of forgiving, but you are aware of being released from a shackle you may not have noticed, experiencing the feeling of being forgiven. There's simply a peace you feel that wasn't there before your déjà vu moment. These fourth-dimension experiences can open your heart to compassion, providing a spiritual view point you didn't see before, such as, "forgive them, for they knew not what they were doing." Until you learn a new way of being, forgive yourself, for you knew not what you were doing.

> **"To forgive is to set a prisoner free, and to discover that prisoner was you. Forgiving does not erase the bitter past. A healed memory is not a deleted memory. Instead, forgiving what we cannot forget creates a new way to remember. We change the memory of our past into a hope for our future."**
>
> —Lewis B. Smedes

34
EDUCATION, HMMM...

I LOVED SCHOOL as a kid. I still love going to school today.
Besides the school of hard knocks, I attained my high school diploma when I was in my mid-twenties. I did this for two reasons:

1. I wanted to set a good example for Devona, my daughter. How could I support my insisting she get a high school education if I didn't have one?
2. Once I acquired a high school education, all sorts of opportunities were open for me.

I went to school for Cattle Management and Breeding because in my late twenties and early thirties I worked on a dairy farm as well as my own pork producing farm. I fell in love with cattle the first time I was up close and personal with them and I wanted to be educated about them. When I became certified in this field, I went back to the female herdswoman there and share what I had learned with her. It was great fun!

I needed a new career living in a new state. I had researched farms in Colorado, and there was no way I was working on a family farm out in the boonies as a single woman. I decided I wanted to work in the beauty industry. That meant I had to go to school and become licensed. I chose nail care and became a licensed nail tech. I had a lot of fun with that. I worked in a high-end salon/spa in Colorado coming right out of school. I landed a position when I came back to Michigan with a summer resort that ranked in the top twenty-five resorts in the world. It was located on an island in the straits of the Great Lakes. Good times all around with that one. Then when the season was over, I came home and milked cows.

The island resort I worked at was about four hundred miles from home, so after two years of working there I decided I wanted to work closer to home. I found a position as a manager of the laundry department in one of the biggest salons in the Flint area. They had a massage school in their building. I received ten percent off my education through the Power of Touch Massage School because I worked in the salon in which it was located. Voila, I added another level of services I could perform for my clients. I learned a lot about energy in our bodies, how it can move, or sometimes become stuck in a place inside us. My practice really took off with that education under my belt.

I had a dream of doing facials since the first time I entered cosmetology school, so I fulfilled that dream, went back to school and became a licensed esthetician. Now, I could do everything in the spa industry except hair, which I had no interest in learning.

With the nail and facial license and a Michigan Massage Therapist Certification, I created a business of my own. I made a beautiful spa in the lower portion of my home and would hire myself out to work retreats. My business was then brick and mortar and mobile. I also worked as freelancer, filling in when salon/spa businesses needed someone to cover when a service provider went on vacation.

Then as I was aging out of the business, I decided to fulfill another dream I had and that was to become an esthetician instructor. I went back to school again and became licensed in that field. I landed a position in one of the top schools in the United States, Douglas J.

In 2017, I retired from the beauty industry and began working in retail, because I had another dream: I wanted to create a successful online retail business. I needed to learn retail. I worked for a hardware store for a year, then the move to Iowa came along. My daughter was to marry Matt, who lived in Iowa and she was moving there to do that, and they insisted that I move too. I sold my properties in Michigan, purchased a home in this state, and spent the first year here remodeling it. I wasn't ready to start my own business here yet, although I had put everything in place for it: DBA, LLC, business bank account, and studied online retail through a mentor who owns the online company, Worldwide Brands.

Once again, I went out and found a position in the Anamosa Walmart Store as Asset Protection which is a team of associates that help prevent shortages through theft and mistakes made at the registers, as well as provide a safe environment for both the shopper and associates. Not only did this provide a nice income but also, I learned about how retail stores promote their inventories. A retail store is in constant change because of sales promotions and season changes. A fabulous learning tool for me when I decided to open an online store. While I was doing this, I went to school with TomBird.com to learn how to properly write my book and get it published. Which is what you are now reading.

I was offered a free Self-Mastery course through one of my friends who needed a practice client for certification as a life coach. I'm currently working the assignments so that I can receive a certification as a life coach.

After almost a year of working at Walmart, I became ready to hire a business coach for my online retail store and work from home. I am currently building a website and have an eBay store. Which is doing pretty well, for only being up about three months.

I have numerous certificates I've attained over the years. I've had to learn the business end of being an online retailer, which required courses in QuickBooks, Time management, Google, Word, and Excel.

I have gone to school to learn about controlling waste materials, computer classes, ministry, Reiki I, 2, and 3. I am a certified Reiki Master. I am also a certified psychic/intuitive.

These are the highlights of my education.

I thoroughly enjoy attaining knowledge.

When I was first diagnosed with bipolar disorder, for five years I studied every book I could get my hands on concerning psychology. I wanted to understand what was going on with my brain chemistry and how it affected my life. I am a natural when it comes to psychology. It's one the talents the Creator endowed me with. The other is a thirst for knowledge.

I knew a long time ago that the world was becoming more demanding and complicated when it came to finding work. One needed to learn how to be creative when it comes to creating an income.

I began teaching Devona at a very early age that a girl in this day and age could not have too many skills. She has also gone to school to gain knowledge of what holds her interest.

Because of being educated, I've had many wonderful experiences and opportunities for personal and professional growth.

Knowledge is power!

35
THE EGO'S USE OF EMOTIONS

Definition of ego: Your sense of identity.
Definition of Indifference: Lack of interest, concern or sympathy, unimportance.

YOUR FUNDAMENTAL BELIEFS, attitudes and feelings may be filtered through the emotion of indifference. Indifference may be part of the identity your ego-mind created in childhood to protect you.

Ask, "Is the feeling, (present), and emotion, (past), of indifference toward myself working in my life today?"

"How do I feel when I'm practicing self-indifference?"

"Does indifference affect my life through love or fear?"

This may be one of many times your ego-mind tempts you to move your focus from gaining loving knowledge to its chattering about what you could do, what you didn't do, what you should do or what someone else did. Why wouldn't it respond this way? You are changing because you are beginning to see clearly. Your ego has established your personal identity and defining itself through the emotions you experienced in childhood. Experiencing lack of interest from others for you, or others not being concerned about you or no show of sympathy for you, doesn't it stand to reason, as a powerless child, that you would become hypnotized into the feeling of unimportance? The ego will use this to its advantage. It will try to tell you that you are different from other people, therefore, "special" and that equals being separated from your Self, and others.

Any strong emotion you carry is used by your ego-mind to keep you in fear and confusion. In the past the ego has been quite indulged through your listening to its voice. You're not doing that so much anymore. As you let go of the feelings and emotions that don't lovingly support you today, you will naturally, a little at a time, become indifferent to the voice of the ego. Make friends with it though, remembering to hold your enemies closer.

Look up definitions of the strongest feelings and emotions you are experiencing in the present. Write down the definitions. Doing this exercise will help you become more deeply connected to your emotional being because you'll be learning its language. It will help you acknowledge on a deep level why and how your ego identity was formed in childhood and what it looks like today.

A few things your ego doesn't want you to recognize is its blaring, blabbering voice, or listening to it with intent to hear its insanity. What the ego is about is providing the illusion of separation from others, your Higher Source, and your Self.

Do your best to focus your attention on your whispering inner voice, it will take you on a plain path, leading you into your promise land.

I have found that having an intention on which to build a life is very important to my successes.

I have been building my life on the foundation of this intention for some time now. It is taken from sentences 6 and 7 of the introduction of *A Course in Miracles:*

"The course does not aim at teaching the meaning of love, for that is beyond what can be taught. It does aim, however, at **removing the blocks to the awareness of love's presence, which is your natural inheritance.**"

This intention of "removing the blocks to the awareness of love's presence," is one of the fundamentals of the foundation of spiritual laws and truths in which I stand in and it serves the common good of all.

When you are focused, grounded in an intention that not only supports your life, but includes the common good of all, you are in a powerful position to crystalize your feelings and thoughts into kind and wondrous encounters through your physical life!

Jesus taught that heaven is within us. I don't know about you, but when I think of heaven being in me, I get goose-bumpy about how I can bring heaven out of me and live my heaven here and now.

Feelings of indifference, entwined with ego identity, is a recipe for living in hell on earth.

Trusting your Source, you can ask it to take any feeling or emotion and transform it into love, however the Higher Power demonstrates that in your life. You can ask to see it through the eyes of your God, ask your Self to provide you with its perception of the feelings you feel. The ego doesn't want you to do this. It pisses it off! Expect resistance for a while.

When we let go of our outdated attitudes and assumptions about ourselves, they take a while to die. They are like chickens or snakes; their bodies still have life after their heads have been cut off. The ego uses their withering, decapitated bodies to trick us into believing they are still very much alive and with us. It's a fear tactic. The ego doesn't like change of any kind. It prefers the status quo.

A woman told me she was experiencing strong suicidal thoughts and feelings. She came up with an exercise that helped her through it. She used lined notebook paper and made three columns on each page. She began with the word "Trust' in the first column. The second column she titled, "The Negative;" the third column was titled, "The Positive."

Under Trust, she wrote what the word means to her. In the negative column, she wrote about what she felt was negative about trusting, and in the positive column she wrote about what she felt was positive about trusting.

She did this with words like honor, peace, love, truth, and so on. She inventoried only positive words.

She was living a pretty good life. She wanted to know where these strong thoughts of suicide were coming from.

This took her three months to complete, working on it almost every day for an hour or so.

Soon after beginning her inventory, her suicide thoughts slowly began to fade. What she was left with was her ego. She discovered that her ego was extremely distorted and diseased in suicide mode. To her, it looked like a giant, dying blob, breathing its last breath. What she learned doing this exercise, is that her ego was trying to convince her to kill herself and convince her that it would go on living! It was attempting to make itself a god, at any expense, including hers and its.

Since having this spiritual insight, she no longer has suicidal thoughts.

Being willing to look your ego-mind straight in the eye will reap the benefit of recognizing it is not your loving source.

The ego's function is to protect you, that's how you made it through your childhood. Now, it needs to stand down, because you are no longer a child, you are an adult, empowered through your true Source!

The ego, your false identity and indifference, the emotion, have much in common. Indifference is another word for fear. Fear of not being valued, cared for, and therefore, feeling

Stillness of Thought

unimportant. The ego uses fear to befuddle us. It teaches separation, as does indifference. Hell can also reside within us. It depends on the choice we make, to which inner voice we listen.

Your ego mind is the talker. It never stops talking.
Your Spirit is the listener.
Your ego is the noisy grasshopper.
Your Spirit is the quiet giant.
Your ego uses your changing body, feelings, and mind to be an expression of itself in the world.
Your Spirit, which is your unchanging self, the "I AM," uses your body, feelings, and mind to be an expression of itself in the world.
Choose wisely which voice you listen to.

36
HOLD YOUR FRIENDS CLOSE, HOLD YOUR ENEMIES CLOSER

PSALMS, CHAPTER 27 tells us to trust the Lord, don't be afraid of what shows up and its last two verses gives directions on how to think and feel about any situation that scares the daylights out of us!

It's a tool you can use to navigate through the fears of traversing the unknown; the inner enemies of fear, depression, and negative self-talk. It describes what can happen to a human being walking this earth and it also offers remedies for overcoming your enemies, which are your thoughts and feelings.

Let's look at Psalms 27

Psalms 27:1 The LORD is my light and my salvation; whom shall I fear? The LORD is the strength of my life; of whom shall I be afraid?

The first question to ask is: "How do I know who my Lord is?"

You may consider it's either your ego or your intuition, depending on which voice you listen to the most.

When you listen to your ego, do you feel uptight?

When you listen to and follow your intuition do you feel lighter? Is your life easier?

If the Lord, Source, Higher Power, Universe, or whatever you choose to call God, is your light, salvation, and strength, why should you be afraid of anything or anyone?

² When the wicked, even mine enemies and my foes, came upon me to eat up my flesh, they stumbled and fell.

The wicked, your enemies and your foes who come upon you to eat up your flesh, are not outside of you! They are the unloving thoughts and feelings you hold against others and yourself.

If you believe your Higher Power or Source is your light, salvation, and strength, kind and caring, why wouldn't your inner foes stumble and fall?

³ Though a host should encamp against me, my heart shall not fear: though war should rise against me, in this will I be confident.

Though a host of unkind and unloving thoughts encamp against you, doesn't it feel like it when you are thinking negatively about any situation you may be in?

While the inner war encamps and revolts against you, your heart doesn't fear; it's confident believing it is the light, salvation, and strength instructing it through intuition.

⁴ One thing have I desired of the Lord, that will I seek after; that I may dwell in the house of the Lord all the days of my life, to behold the beauty of the Lord, and to enquire in his temple.

Look inside yourself and ask, "What's my perception of the beauty of the Lord?" and "Where is the Lord's temple?"

⁵ For in the time of trouble he shall hide me in his pavilion: in the secret of his tabernacle shall he hide me; he shall set me up upon a rock.

In troubles, you are protected in the pavilion, the secret tabernacle, and have been set upon a rock. Where is the pavilion, the secret tabernacle and a rock within you? What does it look like?

⁶ And now shall mine head be lifted up above mine enemies' round about me: therefore, will I offer in his tabernacle sacrifices of joy; I will sing, yea, I will sing praises unto the Lord.

Now that you have entered your vision of your pavilion, the secret tabernacle and sitting on your rock, you can see all around yourself, because your head is lifted above your enemies. You are becoming aware of what your ego-mind is chattering about. It never stops talking. It is always concerned with what you could do, what you didn't do, what you should do and what someone else did.

⁷ Hear, O Lord, when I cry with my voice: have mercy also upon me and answer me.

Now that you have become aware of your ego's messages, call it, "Friend," hold yourself close.

⁸ When thou said, seek ye my face; my heart said unto thee, 'Thy face, Lord, will I seek.'

Ask yourself what does the Lord's face look like to me?

⁹ Hide not thy face far from me; put not thy servant away in anger: thou hast been my help; leave me not, neither forsake me, O God of my salvation.

Do you feel alone, separated from the Power and in fear, do you believe you have been forsaken? Pronounce this enemy, "Friend!" Hold yourself closer.

¹⁰ When my father and my mother forsake me, then the Lord will take me up.

Was there a moment in your childhood that you felt someone was watching over you no matter how wretched the circumstances? You were not forsaken!

¹¹ Teach me thy way, O Lord, and lead me in a plain path, because of mine enemies.

Your ego-mind takes you on rabbit-hole chases, most of your protective friends, your ego-mind defenses, constructed so long ago, have become your enemies. Intuition (which is your Higher Power or Your Higher Self), leads you on a plain path.

¹² Deliver me not over unto the will of mine enemies: for false witnesses are risen up against me, and such as breathe out cruelty.

We are habitual creatures; can you break the habit of listening to the ego's voice and develop the habit of listening to your intuition? The enemy is your ego, fear based self-talk, (false evidence appearing real). It is cruel and deceives you into believing you are separate from your Creator. Ask to be released from the chaos of this moment.

¹³ I had fainted, unless I had believed to see the goodness of the Lord in the land of the living.

Can you see mercy here? After taking a long look at your enemies, you can faint, go back to sleep to the awareness of their presence and intentions. Or can you move the eyes of your heart to focus on the good in your life? Ask, "How far have I come?"

¹⁴ Wait on the Lord: be of good courage, and he shall strengthen thine heart: wait, I say, on the Lord.

You are being given instructions: Do nothing, yet simply wait in gratitude!

Finding gratitude, like forgiveness, comes in levels, like peeling off the layers of an onion. Be patient with the process.

When you pay attention to your thoughts and feelings, you give yourself the power to change the situation through changing your beliefs about yourself. When you make friends with all aspects of yourself, especially the ones you don't like, you become more peaceful inside. This would be unconditional self-love.

Getting to know yourself is like rafting down a spring runoff, with a team beside you, through the mountains, in 32-degree raging waters that peak and curl a few inches in front of your face, splashing their icy coldness over the sides of your inflated raft, as you and your team navigate yourselves through the winding river!

Scary, huh? Yet, so exciting to discover what makes you tick!

37
BITS OF WISDOM ATTAINED ON THE JOURNEY

1. If it wasn't for your birthday; you wouldn't be here. Celebrate your birthday!
2. Believe in a Power greater than yourself.
3. Trust and follow your intuition, it will safely lead you.
4. Sincerely make amends with your children. Deep wounds will heal for all concerned.
5. Relationships we have with others are expressions of love working through us.
6. Live life in gratitude for all that comes onto your path.
7. Giving and receiving are the same. They both bring joy.

8. Always consider the common good of all when making decisions.
9. Make "no" your new "yes" to you.
10. Let go of any expectations you have of others. Expectations bring suffering.
11. Live in integrity, it drastically lowers drama from your life.
12. When you need a pick-me-up, watch comedy. Laughter heals.
13. Trust yourself.
14. Learn to trust all the people in your life for what you can trust them for, the good, the bad, and the ugly. This induces peace.
15. See what you desire to see even if appearances oppose your vision.
16. Don't lie, not even little white ones. They erode your integrity.
17. Listen to the lyrics woven through the melody.
18. Laugh at yourself, especially your ego when it is doing its talk, talk, fear act.
19. Listen for unspoken contracts, then speak them aloud.
20. Hugging a tree is healing and lifts your mood. Hug a tree today.

38
GIVING AND RECEIVING ARE THE SAME

I CONCLUDE *A Stillness of Thought* by passing along to you a gift that was given to me, **The Spiritual Distinction Meditation**. This meditation will help you to consciously differentiate how your ego mind feels and how your spirit feels. Your ego defenses protect you when you can't consciously protect yourself. Your ego-mind isn't bad or evil, it communicates with words, judgments and comparisons. Your Spirit communicates with intuitive feelings.

Meditation is the key to your spiritual practice. It is the highest form of prayer. In it you are so close to God that you don't need to say a thing; it's just great being together.

Our composite parts:

1. **Spirit:** this is life force, your Higher Power, the Knower, the Witness, the Observer, the Perceiver,

Intelligence, Holy Spirit, Christ Consciousness and so on.

2. **Vision:** A spiritually created, three-dimensional holographic image that is telepathically projected from your Spirit though the projector of your Mind for the purpose of creating.

3. **Feelings:** Vibrational frequencies of energy telepathically communicated directly from your Spirit to your body, by-passing your mind.

4. **Mind:** A physical plane tool used to record life's experiences, remembrances, projections, date retention, separation identity, (Ego). Used to formulate plans and strategies to create the future you consciously or unconsciously envision.

5. **Body:** An oxygen-carbon unit, composed of minerals and water, created by Spirit as a machine to function on the earth plane and implement the plans and strategies formulated by your Mind to attain your consciously or unconsciously envisioned future.

Practicing this meditation daily for ninety days will help you be able to FEEL, not think, the difference between your composite parts. It works in conjunction with the Twelve Healing Feelings, page 39. Falling prey to any of the Twelve Emotional Blocks, block what you are really feeling, and keeps you from healing. Healing Feelings are natural, normal and necessary. Emotional Blocks are negative, immature, and dysfunctional.

You need to release repressed feelings that are associated with traumas you have experienced, especially in childhood because what happened to you, really happened.

Record this meditation in your own voice on your cell phone so that you have it handy any time of the day to utilize the Spiritual Distinction Meditation. Be sure to title your recording. If you don't have a recorder on your phone, you can easily download one from Google Play Store or iTunes for an Apple phone.

Spiritual Distinction Meditation

Breath and relax...

Sit comfortably in a chair and close your eyes. Take a moment to consciously declare your intention to "feel" the difference between your Spirit, body, vision, and mind. Then relax and take three long, slow deep breaths, inhaling through your nose to the count of seven, holding your breath to the count of seven and exhaling out of your mouth to the count of seven. As you are doing this, pinpoint your attention on commanding your mind to focus on the difference between how your breath feels when you inhale and how it feels when you exhale.

Feel Your Body Senses...

Listen to the faintest sound you can hear. Take a few more seconds and listen for an even fainter sound. Next, inhale through your nose and notice what you smell, (food, grass, candle, perfume). Now, swish your tongue around inside your mouth and between your gums and notice what you taste, (salty, sour, sweet or bitter). Next feel the skin on the back of your hand between your knuckles and your wrist as lightly as you can. Notice how sensitive your sense of touch actually is. Your skin protects your body in the same way your Ego-Mind protects your psyche, but with one exception: your Ego-Mind is a thousand times more sensitive than your skin.

Feel the Difference Between How Your Body Feels and How Your Spirit Feels

Focus your attention on your body by moving it ... lift your legs, pinch your skin, make a fist and move your head around. Feel how thick, heavy, and solid your body feels. Next, feel your Spirit by rapidly breathing in and out very assertively, rebirthing style, at least three to five times until you create a minor altered state of consciousness by unbalancing your oxygen/carbon dioxide gases. Doing this correctly should feel mildly uncomfortable. As you exhale your last breath, try not to breathe for ten seconds. Now, just feel what you are feeling; this is your Spirit. Feel how the light vibration of Spirit feels. Now, feel the difference between how your Spirit feels and how your body feels, make a fist, which will bring your attention back to your body, so that you can compare how different they feel. Pause for ten seconds to feel the difference.

Feel the Difference Between How Your Body Feels and How Your Vision Feels

Pick a vision that easy for you to visualize, like a car, house, person, or beach. Create it with as much detail as possible. Make the vision so real that you can pick up something and feel that it has weight. Now smell it and put it against your skin and feel its temperature. Notice that in your vision you perceive height, depth, width, sound, weight, temperature, and even odor. Feel your body again, actually feel it, make a fist. Feel how similar your body and vision feel. Lastly, feel the subtle difference between the weight of the molecules of your body and the weight of the molecules in your vision, which is much lighter. Pause for ten seconds and feel the difference.

Feel the Difference Between How Your Ego-Mind Feels and How Your Spirit Feels

Next, notice that your mind is always sub-vocalizing, talking in your head. Notice what your mind is saying right now. Pause and listen. Be sure to catch what your mind is saying. Do not accept a general answer like, "My mind is quiet." This is usually an indication that you can't distinguish between your Intuitive Self and your mind talk. Your mind never stops talking. It's always concerned with what you should be doing, what you didn't do, what you could do, and what someone else did, Talk, talk, and talk! Your mind is addicted to excitement and you can usually feel it in your stomach area, like when you go down the first hill of a roller coaster and feel that, "Woooooooh" feeling. Now just feel how you feel when your Ego-Mind is doing its think-think-fear act. Feel your ego's uptight, stressful energy, pause to feel it. Next, repeat the same procedures you did to feel Spirit by breathing rapidly in and out, very assertively at least three to five times until you create a minor, altered state of consciousness. When you exhale your last breath, do nothing but feel your Spirit. Feel the quiet, light vibration of Spirit. Now, focus your attention on feeling the difference between how your Spirit feels and how your Ego-Mind feels. Notice that your Ego-Mind is the talker and your Spirit is the listener. Pause here for about ten seconds to feel the difference. Spend a few minutes in this state of bliss by focusing your "feelings" on the different sensations of inhaling and exhaling. Then when you feel complete, open your eyes.

This meditation has power in and of itself to change your life. Take the time to study, practice, internalize, and emotionalize the Spiritual Distinction Meditation until it becomes a part of your consciousness.

EPILOGUE

After a while I looked in the mirror and realized ... wow, after all those hurts, scars, and bruises, after all those trials, I really made it through. I did it. I became who I wanted to be! I survived that which was supposed to kill me. So, I straightened my crown ... and walked away like a queen.

Peace be with you!
K.D. Cannon
July 22, 2020

ACKNOWLEDGEMENTS

This book was written with the loving support of many folks throughout my journey into healing of the wounds of victimization in childhood through domestic violence, abandonment, physical, emotional, and sexual abuse. This is my opportunity to acknowledge and thank you all for your assistance in lifting my consciousness out of the attitudes and feelings of victimhood.

To the orphanage on Cedar Street, thank you for providing me with shelter, food, a warm bed, clothing, primary education, protection, and safety when I was in danger.

After years of separation, thank you, Wilson Foster, for the hours, days, weeks, months, and years you were a nurturing father and grandfather to me and your granddaughter.

To Devona Muday, who walked this journey with me all her life, thank you. I love you with all my heart!

Thank you to my best friends, Linda Jacobi, Susan Miller, and Sabrina Saeidifar, for your faith in me to create the life of my dreams.

To all the doctors and counselors in secular psychology who gave of their time and talents to heal my mind, thank you. A special thank you goes out to Eric Enbody. He was my first teacher to guide and instruct me in the ways of changing my thinking.

Thank you to Unity for introducing me to Spiritual laws and truths that provided me with the nourishment I needed to plant myself and grow roots.

Mary Ellen Wojie, a big thank you goes out to you! You suggested I write this book and you suggested Tom Bird's publishing program. And here we are!

A special thank you to Tom Bird and his staff at Sojourn Publishing for their direction and support in getting *A Stillness of Thought* in book form. Thank you, Donna Velasco, for talking me through some of the challenges of writing this book.

To St. Paul's Lutheran church, thank you for your warm welcome into this new community.

To all the luminaries that wrote their books to teach and encourage all beings how to live life with intention, thank you.

Contact Kathleen at astillnessofthought@gmail.com

REFERENCES

Holy Bible	King James Version
Psychiatric Dictionary 4th Edition	Leland E. Hensie, M.D.; Robert J. Campbell, M.D.
Dictionary of Behavioral Science	1973 Compiled and edited by Benjamin B. Wolman
Mania-An Evolving Concept	Edited by Robert H. Belmaker, M.D.
The Sky's the Limit	Dr. Wayne Dyer
Power of Intention	Dr. Wayne Dyer
Wishes Fulfilled: Mastering the Art of Manifesting	Dr. Wayne Dyer
The Power of Now: A Guide to Spiritual Enlightenment	Eckhart Tolle
Mood Swings	John Mac Arthur Jr
I Never Promised You a Rose Garden	Hannah Green

Secret Scars- A Guide for Survivors of Child Sexual Abuse	Cynthia Crosson Tower
Scream Louder	Marsh Utain & Barbara Oliver
The Greatest Miracle in the World	Og Mandino
The Science of Mind	Ernest S. Holmes
The Complete Reader	Neville Goddard
A Course in Miracles	Published by the foundation for Inner Peace
You Are a Badass; How to Stop Doubting Your Greatness & Start Living an Awesome Life	Jen Sincero
Love and Law	Ernest Holmes, 1887-1960
Lessons in Truth	H. Emilie Cady
The Four Agreements	Miguel Angel Ruiz, M.D.
The Mastery of Love	Miguel Angel Ruiz, M.D.
The Power of Your Subconscious Mind	Joseph Murphy Ph.D., D.D.
You Can Heal Your Life	Louise L. Hay
The Untethered Soul	Michael A. Singer
The Wisdom of Wallace d. Wattles II	Copyright 2007 BN Publishing
The Invitation	Oriah Mountain Dreamer
A Course of Love Combined Volume	Mari Perron, First Receiver
The Writings of Florence Scovel Shinn	Includes the Shinn Biography
The Presence of Magical Thinking	Einstein DA, Menzies RG.

Bruno Bettelheim (1977)	In children a magical belief is fuel for imaginary role-play and fantasizing that helps children to cope with the chaos of June 2004 338 The Psychologist Vol 17 No 6
Developing of a Child's Brain	https://www.firstthingsfirst.org
Magical Thinking-Pre-school educators: Susan A. Miller Ed.D. 9/17/2020 Ellen Booth Church, and Carla Poole https://www.scholastic.com/teachers/articles-content/ages-stages-how-children-use-magical-thinking 9/17/2020	https://www.scholastic.com/teachers
- Dale Carnegie	https://www.brainyquote.com/search_results?q=Dale+carnegie+magical+thinking 9/17/2020
Codependency No More	Melody Beattie
Who Would You Be Without Your Story	Bryon Katie
The Daily Word	Unity
The Surrender Experiment	Michael S. Singer
Think and Grow Rich	Napoleon Hill
A New Earth: Awakening to Your Life's Purpose	Eckhart Tolle
Songs of Spirit Albums	Karen Drucker
Nurturing Your Inner Child (Meditation CD)	Steven Halpern
Love is Letting Go of Fear	Gerald G. Jampolsky
Alcoholics Anonymous	Alcoholics Anonymous World Service 1976

www.ingramcontent.com/pod-product-compliance
Lightning Source LLC
Chambersburg PA
CBHW071451080526
44587CB00014B/2070